The Anatomy of 7 Vows

OrangeBooks Publication

1st Floor, Rajhans Arcade, Mall Road, Kohka, Bhilai, Chhattisgarh 490020
Website: **www.orangebooks.in**

First Edition, 2025

ISBN: 978-93-7426-164-4

Price: Rs. 350.00

Printed in India

THE ANATOMY OF 7 VOWS

It's not just love, it's the VOWS that bind -
let's break down the secrets of happy marriage

MAJOR (DR.) NAVJEET KAUR

OrangeBooks Publication
www.orangebooks.in

Preface

Marriage is one of the most beautiful journeys two souls can take together. Yet, in today's world, it is also one of the most vulnerable. Every day, I meet individuals and couples who began their relationships with love in their eyes and dreams in their hearts, but who now struggle with pain, distance, or even the thought of giving up.

The purpose of this book is simple yet profound: **to save marriages, to heal hearts, and to bring enlightenment to relationships.**

We live in an age of instant gratification, where patience runs thin, distractions are endless, and the pressures of work, finances, and societal expectations weigh heavily on couples. Too often, marriages collapse not because of a lack of love, but because of a lack of understanding, communication, and guidance.

I believe the wisdom we need has always been with us. The **seven vows of marriage**—spoken around the sacred fire in Hindu tradition—are not just rituals of the past. They are living principles that can guide us through the storms of the present. They remind us of what truly matters: nourishment, support, discipline, resilience, shared purpose, family, and lifelong companionship.

This book was born from my deep desire to help couples rediscover these truths—not as ancient words, but as daily practices. Each chapter is woven with real-life stories, psychological insights, reflection questions, and practical exercises. My intention is to make the vows **accessible, relatable, and alive** for couples of all backgrounds.

If this book can help even one couple step back from the edge of separation, choose love over resentment, or remember why they chose each other in the first place, then my mission will feel fulfilled.

To those who read these pages: I invite you to walk with an open heart. Allow these vows to guide you, to heal you, and to remind you that love is not a destination but a journey—one that requires care, commitment, and courage.

May this book not only save marriages but also **enlighten hearts**, showing us all that the true essence of marriage is not perfection, but persistence. Not losing yourself, but finding a deeper meaning in togetherness.

✨ *This is my offering—from my heart to yours—in the hope that more marriages blossom into the sacred partnerships they were always meant to be.*

Contents

Introduction – The Timeless Dance of Love and Commitment 1

Chapter - 1
Marriage Across Cultures and Faiths 9

Chapter - 2
Stages of a Relationship 18

Chapter - 3
Symbols of Marriage: Agni, the Number 7, and Varmala 27

Chapter 4
The First Vow: Nourishment and Stability 35

Chapter - 5
The Second Vow: Emotional and Spiritual Support 44

Chapter - 6
The Third Vow: Commitment to Self-Discipline and Action 52

Chapter - 7
The Fourth Vow: Resilience and Handling Setbacks 60

Chapter - 8
The Fifth Vow: Purposeful Living and Legacy 68

Chapter - 9

The Sixth Vow: Nurturing Family and Children..........76

Chapter - 10

The Seventh Vow: Lifelong Companionship & Friendship..........84

Chapter - 11

Challenges to the Seven Vows in Modern Marriages ...92

Chapter - 12

Practical Ways to Renew and Revisit the Vows in Modern Life..........101

Chapter - 13

Navigating Extended Family and Intercaste Marriages Through the Seven Vows 109

Chapter - 14

Modern Rituals and Alternative Ways to Express the Seven Vows 118

Chapter - 15

Real-Life Case Studies of Couples Living (or Struggling With) the Seven Vows..........126

Chapter - 16

A Guide for Couples to Create Their Own Personalized Vows..........134

Chapter - 17

The Role of Forgiveness and Healing in Honoring the Vows..........142

Chapter - 18

Communication as the Lifeline of the Vows 150

Chapter - 19

Intimacy and Romance as Expressions of the Vows .. 158

Chapter - 20

Conflict as a Pathway to Deeper Understanding........ 166

Chapter - 21

Parenting, Partnership, and the Seven Vows.............. 175

Chapter - 22

Balancing Individuality and Togetherness in Marriage 184

Compatibility and Understanding Partner's Mind (Multiple Choice).. 195

Introduction – The Timeless Dance of Love and Commitment

Are we in the right relationship?

Will we truly stay together forever?

Is the person I love really the right one for me?

What will our life look like after marriage?

Are we truly compatible?

If these questions have ever touched your heart, know that you are not alone. They are the silent whispers that almost every couple carries at some point—before the wedding, during the early years, or even decades later when life's storms arrive.

Marriage is one of the most profound journeys we undertake as human beings. It is not just the coming together of two people—it is the weaving of two stories, two families, sometimes even two cultures or faiths, into a single fabric of love and shared destiny.

And yet, in today's world, this fabric often feels fragile. The pressures of work, financial responsibilities, shifting gender roles, societal expectations, and the constant buzz of technology strain the threads that hold relationships together. Many couples find themselves deeply in love yet struggling to stay connected.

Why This Book, Why Now?

The idea of this book was born from a simple yet powerful realization: the ancient vows of marriage still hold extraordinary wisdom for modern couples.

In Hindu tradition, these vows—the *Saptapadi* or **seven sacred steps**—are spoken around a sacred fire. But their essence goes far beyond ritual. They are **universal principles** of love, commitment, and partnership. Whether spoken in Sanskrit thousands of years ago or reimagined in modern language today, they capture the deepest truths of what makes relationships thrive.

- To provide for and nourish each other.
- To offer emotional and spiritual support.
- To live with discipline, respect, and shared responsibility.
- To stay resilient through hardships.
- To live with purpose and leave a legacy.
- To nurture family and community with love.
- To walk together as lifelong companions and friends.

This book reinterprets these vows for **modern marriages**—not just in India, but across cultures and contexts. It shows how they can guide us not only on the wedding day but every single day that follows.

The Reality of Relationships Today — Indian Insights

Marriage in India is still considered sacred, but the pressures of modern life are making it harder to sustain. Studies across the country reveal what many couples already feel in their hearts. Let's look at what the research says—explained in simple words.

1. Emotions Decide the Quality of Marriage

A study in Bangalore found that couples with **high emotional intelligence**—the ability to stay calm, understand each other's feelings, and handle stress—were far happier in their marriages. Those who struggled with anger or stress often felt dissatisfied.

☞ *Simple truth:* **If you can manage your emotions and listen to your partner with empathy, your marriage grows stronger every day.**

2. Family Involvement — A Double-Edged Sword

In Delhi, researchers discovered that families play a huge role in marital happiness. When families were supportive, couples felt secure and loved. But when families interfered too much, tension and unhappiness followed.

☞ *Simple truth:* **Families can be a backbone or a burden. The key is balance—love without interference.**

3. Money and Stability Matter

A study in rural Uttar Pradesh showed that men from financially stable families were about **three times more likely to report a happy marriage** compared to those with financial struggles.

☞ *Simple truth:* **Money may not buy love, but it removes daily stress and creates space for affection and peace.**

4. Loneliness Inside Marriage

A 2024 study of more than a thousand married Indians found something surprising: **almost half still felt lonely in their marriage.** Many said they had little emotional connection with their spouse, and more than half rated their marriage as poor in quality.

☞ *Simple truth:* **Marriage is not just living under the same roof. True connection needs daily care—talking, sharing, laughing, and listening.**

5. Personality Shapes Marriage

Another study found that people who were **calm, caring, and dependable** enjoyed better marriages. On the other hand, those who were very anxious, moody, or quick-tempered often struggled to maintain harmony.

☞ *Simple truth:* **Your nature matters—patience, kindness, and stability are silent pillars of a strong marriage.**

6. Intimacy is Essential

In Kerala, researchers found that **intimacy and closeness were directly linked to happiness in marriage**, especially for men. Without affection and emotional warmth, even marriages that looked fine from outside felt empty inside.

☞ *Simple truth:* **Intimacy—both emotional and physical—is not a luxury in marriage, it's a necessity.**

Bringing It All Together

These Indian studies show us the reality of modern marriages:

- Couples are not unhappy because they don't love each other, but because **they don't always know how to nurture love daily**.
- Emotional skills, family dynamics, financial stability, and intimacy all play a role in marital satisfaction.
- Many couples silently feel lonely, even when living together.

This is exactly why the **seven vows** are still so powerful. They are not just rituals from the past, but guiding principles for today:

- To provide stability.
- To support each other emotionally.

- To show patience and discipline.
- To stay resilient in hard times.
- To build a purposeful life together.
- To balance family ties with love.
- To walk as companions, hand in hand, for life.

What This Book Offers You

This book is both a reflection and a guide. It blends:

- **Stories of real couples**—some thriving, some struggling—to illustrate how vows play out in daily life.
- **Psychological insights** from emotional intelligence, attachment theory, and modern relationship research.
- **Practical tools, checklists, and exercises** you and your partner can try immediately.
- **Reflection prompts and journaling questions** to spark honest conversations.
- **Alternative rituals and practices** for intercaste, interfaith, and modern couples to make the vows their own.

My goal is not just for you to understand the seven vows, but to **live them**—to let them become daily anchors of nourishment, support, resilience, and companionship in your unique journey.

Marriage as a Living Journey

Marriage is not a one-time event sealed by rituals or paperwork. It is a living, breathing journey. Like a garden, it needs tending—sunlight, water, care, and patience. Left neglected, it withers. Nurtured with love and intention, it blossoms into something extraordinary, offering shade and beauty not only to the couple but also to the generations that follow.

The vows are not chains that restrict us. They are **lights that guide us**—through everyday joys, misunderstandings, reconciliations, and shared dreams. They remind us that love is not only about passion, but about persistence. Not about never falling, but about always rising—together.

An Invitation

As you step into these chapters, take pauses. Reflect. Journal. Try the exercises with your partner. Discuss the questions with honesty and openness.

Whether you are newly married, considering marriage, or decades into your relationship, this book will remind you:

- Love is not just a feeling—it is a practice.
- Commitment is not about perfection—it is about choosing each other, again and again.
- The seven vows are not only ancient words—they are living principles that can carry you through a lifetime.

✨ *This book is not just about marriage. It is about love as a daily choice, companionship as a lifelong gift, and the possibility of building a relationship that is strong, nurturing, and timeless.*

Chapter – 1

Marriage Across Cultures and Faiths

Marriage is one of humanity's oldest and most enduring institutions. Long before nations existed, before industries rose, and before modern society took shape, humans sought companionship, community, and continuity through the union of two individuals. This sacred bond has been celebrated in every culture—whether through rituals before fire, vows in a church, songs in a tribal gathering, or the signatures on a civil contract.

Though the ceremonies differ, the underlying values remain universal: **companionship, love, respect, and shared responsibility.** In this chapter, we will explore how different traditions have understood marriage, and how those lessons continue to guide modern couples navigating today's fast-changing world.

Hinduism: A Sacred Union of Souls

In Hindu philosophy, marriage is not merely a social arrangement—it is a sacred journey. The couple unites to fulfill **dharma (duty), artha (prosperity), kama (desire), and moksha (spiritual liberation).** The seven vows, or *Saptapadi*, form the heart of this sacred bond. Each vow is taken around *Agni*—the sacred fire—which symbolizes purity, divine witness, and transformation.

Traditionally, the vows emphasized roles where the husband was the provider and the wife the nurturer. Today, however, couples reinterpret these promises in light of equality, shared responsibility, and emotional partnership.

❢ **Daily Life Connection:** Think of a couple like Aarav and Meera, both software engineers in Bengaluru. While juggling demanding jobs, they also care for Aarav's aging parents. They see their daily caregiving not as a burden, but as a sacred part of their marriage—living their vows not only in the temple but in the small choices of everyday life.

Christianity: Marriage as Covenant

In Christianity, marriage is seen as a sacrament—a holy covenant between two people and God, symbolizing the union of Christ and the Church. The vows—"for better or worse, for richer or poorer, in sickness and in health"— emphasize permanence, selflessness, and unconditional love.

For Christian couples, prayer, forgiveness, and grace are the foundations of resilience. Marriage is not about avoiding trials but about **walking through them together with faith.**

✨ **Illustrative Story:** Anna and James from Kerala had been married for 25 years when they renewed their vows. Over those years, they faced job losses, miscarriages, and health struggles. Yet, through prayer and mutual forgiveness, they discovered that their love wasn't about perfection but about persistence. James once told their children: *"A strong marriage is built on two people who choose forgiveness daily."*

Islam: Marriage as Partnership

In Islam, *Nikah* (marriage) is both a legal contract and a spiritual commitment. Spouses are described in the Quran as *"garments for each other"*—symbols of comfort, protection, and dignity. Both husband and wife have clear rights and responsibilities, emphasizing **mutual respect, fairness, and compassion.**

In practice, modern Muslim couples often divide household and financial responsibilities based on practicality rather than gender tradition.

❢ **Daily Life Example:** In Dubai, Yasir and Hiba decided early in their marriage to manage their roles by strength: Yasir loves cooking, while Hiba excels at finances. Their friends teased them for "role reversal," but they laugh it off, knowing their partnership thrives because it's built on fairness, not stereotypes.

Judaism: A Covenant of Responsibility

Jewish marriage, or *Kiddushin*, is a covenant witnessed by traditions such as signing the *Ketubah*—a contract that outlines financial and emotional commitments. This act transforms love into responsibility, grounding the couple in accountability.

For Jewish couples, marriage is also deeply tied to community and continuity. Raising children, celebrating festivals, and honouring traditions together bind couples to something larger than themselves.

✿ **Reflection:** The *Ketubah* is a reminder for all couples—across faiths—that commitments written and spoken aloud strengthen accountability. Modern partners might adapt this by writing their own marriage "contract" or vision statement.

Buddhism: Marriage as Mutual Growth

Buddhism does not view marriage as a religious duty but as a moral partnership. The focus is on **mindfulness, compassion, and reducing suffering.** A Buddhist marriage encourages each partner to see the relationship as a path toward spiritual growth.

✨ **Illustrative Story:** A monk once told a newly married couple: *"Do not ask, 'How can my partner make me happy?' Ask instead, 'How can I make my partner's journey lighter?'"* This shift—from receiving to giving—creates marriages grounded in compassion.

Sikhism: Marriage as Anand Karaj (Blissful Union)

In Sikhism, marriage is a union of equals. The ceremony, called *Anand Karaj* ("blissful union"), emphasizes **love, equality, and spiritual companionship.** Sikh philosophy rejects domination of one over the other—both partners are seen as walking together toward divine truth.

❗ **Daily Life Example:** A Sikh couple running a business in Amritsar balances entrepreneurship with parenting and prayer. They see their marriage as teamwork—not just for profit or survival, but as a way to walk closer to God together.

Modern Secular and Cross-Cultural Marriages

Not all marriages today are rooted in religion. Civil marriages, interfaith unions, and intercultural partnerships are increasingly common. These couples often create their own rituals—exchanging handwritten vows, planting a tree together, or creating family mission statements.

🌍 **Case Study:** Rohan, a Hindu, and Sara, a Christian, married in a simple courthouse ceremony. Instead of choosing one religion's rituals, they created their own: every anniversary, they write letters to each other about the year's highs and lows. Over time, those letters have become their most treasured tradition—a testament that rituals need not be ancient to be sacred.

Universal Threads Across Cultures

Despite differences, every tradition echoes four timeless truths:

- **Commitment**: Marriage is a long-term bond, not a temporary arrangement.
- **Mutual respect**: Each partner is valued and honored.
- **Support**: Emotional, financial, and spiritual support are at the heart of the union.

- **Growth**: A true marriage helps both individuals evolve—personally and spiritually.

Reflection Questions

1. What does marriage mean to me beyond rituals and ceremonies?
2. Which values—love, respect, companionship, responsibility—resonate most with my beliefs?
3. How do I see my relationship contributing to my personal and spiritual growth?

Write your reflections below.

Exercises for Couples

1. **Our Marriage Vision Statement:** Sit with your partner and write a one-paragraph vision for your marriage. Example prompts:
    - "In our marriage, we will always…"
    - "We promise to…"
    - "Our union will be a place of…" Revisit this statement every anniversary.
2. **Shared Ritual Design:** Create one small ritual unique to your marriage—lighting a candle before meals, sharing one gratitude daily, or planting a flower together each month.
3. **Intercultural Learning:** If you and your partner come from different backgrounds, spend time learning one another's traditions. Try cooking each other's cultural food or celebrating a festival together.

Closing Thought

Marriage is not defined by the rituals we perform on a single day—it is defined by the meaning we create every day after. Whether before a sacred fire, in a church, under a canopy, or in a courthouse, the essence is the same: two people promising to walk together through the joys, storms, and quiet moments of life.

The real power of marriage lies not in similarity but in harmony—two individuals, sometimes different in faith, personality, or culture, yet choosing to weave their lives together with love, respect, and commitment.

Chapter – 2

Stages of a Relationship

Every love story begins with spark and promise. The flutter of a message notification, the long phone calls, the quiet walks—these small moments weave the early fabric of intimacy. Yet, love is not static. Relationships evolve through different stages, each bringing unique joys and challenges.

Understanding these stages allows couples to prepare for transitions rather than panic when the "honeymoon phase" fades or when conflicts arise. It normalizes the ups and downs and helps couples view challenges not as endings, but as stepping stones.

Stage 1: The Honeymoon Phase

The early stage of love feels intoxicating. Dopamine and oxytocin flood the brain, making partners idealize each other. Everything feels magical—conversations stretch late into the night, and differences seem charming rather than irritating.

Emotions: Excitement, passion, hope.

Challenges: Ignoring red flags, avoiding tough conversations, projecting fantasies.

❢ **Daily Life Example:** Priya and Arjun met in college. They spent hours on the phone, skipping meals and sleep. Arjun's spending habits—lavish dinners, impulsive shopping—seemed romantic to Priya at first. But once they married, those same habits triggered financial tension.

☞ **Lesson:** Infatuation is beautiful, but long-term love requires honesty and financial awareness.

Stage 2: Discovery and Adjustment

The glow of infatuation gives way to reality. Partners begin to notice quirks and imperfections: different routines, habits, and values. This stage requires flexibility, compromise, and communication.

Emotions: Joy mixed with irritation; comfort mingled with conflict.

Challenges: Adjusting to differences, navigating expectations.

✨ **Illustrative Story:** Ravi loved order—shoes in place, dishes washed immediately. Neha, more carefree, left clothes on chairs and books half-open. Their home became a battleground until Ravi learned to let go of smaller irritations, and Neha made efforts toward tidiness. Their willingness to meet halfway transformed tension into teamwork.

Stage 3: The Power Struggle

This is often the most turbulent stage. Partners clash over deeper values: money, family expectations, parenting, or career goals. Power struggles are natural—they test whether the relationship has the resilience to survive conflict.

Emotions: Frustration, defensiveness, disappointment.

Challenges: Poor conflict resolution, blame, risk of separation.

❢ **Case Study:** Sonia wanted to save money for a house; Raj dreamed of launching a startup. Their fights grew heated, with each accusing the other of being selfish. Before long, they considered separation. Counseling taught them to replace accusations ("You never care about security") with "I" statements ("I feel anxious when we don't save"). This shift turned battles into conversations.

☞ **Lesson:** Conflict is not the enemy—poor communication is.

Stage 4: Stability and Trust

Couples who survive power struggles find balance. They learn to respect boundaries and accept differences. Trust deepens, and routines create comfort.

Emotions: Security, predictability, calm.

Challenges: Avoiding monotony, keeping intimacy alive.

✨ **Illustrative Story:** Kavita and Mohan, married for 10 years, noticed they were becoming "roommates." To reignite connection, they created rituals—Friday date nights, Sunday family walks, and "no-phone dinners." These small habits kept their bond fresh.

Stage 5: Commitment and Partnership

Here, partners see each other as true teammates. They plan long-term goals—raising children, buying homes, or building businesses. Decisions are made jointly, with an emphasis on loyalty and teamwork.

Emotions: Loyalty, deep connection, shared vision.

Challenges: Balancing autonomy with partnership.

💡 **Daily Life Example:** When Meera was offered a promotion in another city, Sameer adjusted his freelance career to support her move. Their commitment wasn't about sacrifice but about shared success.

Stage 6: Growth and Intimacy

Couples move beyond logistics into deeper connection—emotional, physical, and spiritual. They support each other's dreams and celebrate victories.

Emotions: Gratitude, joy, mutual pride.

Challenges: Balancing individual ambitions with shared goals.

✨ **Story:** Nisha dreamed of writing a book. Her husband Amit took over evening chores so she had time. When her manuscript was published, Amit celebrated as if it were his own success. Their marriage grew because they invested in each other's growth.

Stage 7: Transformation or Rebirth

This is the mature stage, often reached later in life. The relationship becomes less about proving love and more about living it daily. Couples find joy in companionship and shared history.

Emotions: Peace, unconditional respect, companionship.

Challenges: Adjusting to aging, empty nests, health issues.

💡 **Daily Life Example:** At 65, Suresh and Anjali spend evenings gardening. They've survived financial struggles, raised children, and faced illnesses. Now, they find joy in simple togetherness—the quiet laughter, shared tea, and unspoken understanding of a lifetime walked side by side.

Psychological Insights on Stages

- **Attachment Theory:** Couples with secure attachment navigate transitions more smoothly.
- **The "U-Curve" of Marriage:** Studies show satisfaction often dips during midlife (work and parenting stress) but rises again in later years.

- **Conflict Resolution Styles:** Couples who learn to "fight fair" (listening, validating, compromising) often emerge stronger.

Reflection Questions

1. Which stage best describes our relationship right now?
2. What challenges have we successfully overcome together?
3. How do we nurture intimacy and excitement at this stage?
4. What habits might help us transition to the next stage?

Write your reflections below.

Exercises for Couples

1. **Our Relationship Timeline:** Draw a timeline marking milestones—first meeting, first trip, first fight, wedding, children, etc. Identify which stage you were in during each milestone.

2. **Conflict Style Quiz:** Write down your default style in conflicts: avoidant, aggressive, compromising, or collaborative. Share and discuss how these styles affect your relationship.

3. **Ritual of Connection:** Create one shared ritual (e.g., morning coffee together, weekly gratitude exchange, evening walks). Rituals act as anchors during stressful transitions.

Closing Thought

Relationships are not linear—they circle, bend, and sometimes revisit earlier phases. A couple may feel like newlyweds again during a vacation, or slip into a power struggle when faced with financial stress. What matters is not avoiding these shifts but embracing them as natural seasons.

The beauty of marriage lies in growth—not in being unchanged, but in evolving together. If two people can hold hands through discovery, struggle, and transformation, they discover that love is not just a feeling. It is a journey of becoming—together.

Chapter - 3

Symbols of Marriage: Agni, the Number 7, and Varmala

Rituals are more than customs—they are the poetry of tradition. In every marriage ceremony, symbols are used not only to bless the couple but to remind them of timeless truths. In Hindu weddings, three key symbols stand out: **Agni (sacred fire), the Number 7 (Saptapadi), and the Varmala (exchange of garlands).**

When reinterpreted for modern life, these symbols offer practical wisdom for couples navigating everyday realities.

Agni – The Sacred Witness

In Hindu weddings, vows are taken in the presence of *Agni*, the sacred fire. Fire represents purity, divine presence, and transformation.

🔥 Symbolism of Agni

- Burns away negativity, symbolizing a fresh start.
- Stands as a witness, reminding couples of accountability.
- Provides light and warmth, symbolizing guidance and protection.

❢ **Daily Life Connection:** Fire is more than flames—it is awareness. For modern couples, Agni can be seen as honesty in communication. Each time we speak truthfully or listen with openness, we keep the sacred fire alive in our relationship.

✨ **Illustrative Story:** Ravi and Sunita began a weekly ritual: every Sunday evening, they lit a candle and shared one truth about their week—something they feared, something they celebrated, or something they struggled with. That small flame became their *Agni*, a reminder that vulnerability keeps love strong.

☞ **Modern Insight:** Agni reminds us that marriages don't collapse from grand betrayals alone—they weaken through daily silences, unspoken resentments, and ignored truths. Lighting the "fire of openness" keeps relationships alive.

The Number 7 – Completeness and Wholeness

Why seven vows and not five or ten? Across cultures, the number seven symbolizes completeness:

- 7 days of the week
- 7 colors of the rainbow
- 7 chakras in the human body
- 7 seas and 7 continents

In marriage, seven steps symbolize a complete journey—covering nourishment, prosperity, companionship, loyalty, family, growth, and friendship.

🌈 **Daily Life Reflection:** Just as missing one color weakens a rainbow, ignoring even one vow—such as respect or companionship—weakens a marriage.

✨ **Exercise: The Seven Check-In:** Once a month, sit with your partner and ask these seven questions:

1. Are we nourishing each other?

2. Are we emotionally supporting each other?
3. Are we prospering together?
4. Are we protecting one another?
5. Are we nurturing family and responsibilities?
6. Are we growing together?
7. Are we still best friends?

☞ **Lesson:** This simple ritual ensures couples don't wait for crises to reflect; they course-correct continuously.

Varmala – The Garland of Acceptance

The *Varmala*—the exchange of garlands—represents acceptance, surrender, and humility. By placing flowers on each other, couples agree to:

- Accept each other fully, with flaws and strengths.
- Honor each other with respect.
- Let go of ego to make space for partnership.

✿ **Symbolism of Flowers:** Flowers wilt unless nurtured. Similarly, relationships need constant renewal—freshness, fragrance, and care.

✨ **Illustrative Story:** At their wedding, Priya playfully raised her garland high, making her groom jump to reach it. Years later, whenever they fought, she would laugh and say, *"Remember how hard you had to work to win me over? Marriage is the same—you have to keep trying."* Humor transformed their garland exchange into a lifelong reminder that love requires daily effort.

Modern-Day Applications of Symbols

- **Agni as Transparency:** Light a candle before big conversations as a symbol of honesty.
- **Seven Steps as Ritual:** Do a monthly "7 vows check-in."
- **Varmala as Renewal:** Exchange small tokens (flowers, notes, or even inside jokes) regularly to reaffirm acceptance.

❢ **Case Study – Creating Modern Rituals:** An interfaith couple in Mumbai couldn't agree on which traditions to follow. So, they created their own: every anniversary, they plant a sapling together. For them, the plant symbolizes both *Agni* (growth through nourishment), the *Number 7* (seven years of care for one tree), and *Varmala* (acceptance of shared responsibility).

Psychological Insights

- **Symbolism Builds Memory:** Rituals create "anchors" that couples remember during conflict.
- **Repetition Strengthens Bonds:** Studies show couples who engage in shared rituals report higher satisfaction.

- **Humility and Ego:** Varmala teaches the psychological truth that marriages thrive when both partners occasionally "bow" in compromise.

Reflection Questions

1. What does "fire" mean in our relationship—honesty, passion, or awareness?
2. Which of the seven vows feels strongest in our marriage? Which needs attention?
3. How do we show acceptance daily—beyond words spoken years ago?

Write your reflections below.

Couple's Exercises

1. **Our Sacred Candle:** Choose one evening weekly to light a candle and share one truth from your week—no matter how small.
2. **Rainbow Journal:** Create a journal with seven sections for each vow. Write one example weekly of how you lived that vow.
3. **Flower Exchange:** Every month, exchange something simple—a flower, a note, a small gift—that symbolizes continued acceptance.

Closing Thought

Agni, the Number 7, and Varmala are not relics of the past. They are timeless metaphors, reminding us that marriage is both ritual and reality. Fire teaches honesty, seven vows teach balance, and garlands teach humility.

When couples reinterpret these symbols in daily life, their relationship becomes more than routine—it becomes sacred. Every meal shared, every compromise made, every laughter exchanged becomes a step around the eternal fire, a vow renewed, and a garland offered again.

Chapter 4

The First Vow: Nourishment and Stability

Marriage is built not on grand gestures but on the simple, daily acts of nourishment—food cooked with care, a hand offered in comfort, a shared financial plan, or a word of encouragement after a long day. The **first vow of Hindu marriage** emphasizes nourishment and stability, reminding couples that survival and fulfillment require partnership in both material and emotional realms.

Traditionally, this vow centered on the husband providing food and security, and the wife managing the household. But in today's world, where both partners contribute in varied ways, nourishment extends beyond bread and butter—it includes **mental peace, emotional connection, and spiritual well-being.**

Traditional Meaning of the First Vow

The couple pledges before the sacred fire:

"Together, we will nourish each other and provide for our household with food, wealth, and prosperity. We promise to work for the good of our family and ensure its well-being."

In its essence, this vow is not only about provision but about shared commitment to build a safe, secure, and nurturing life.

Modern Interpretation: Shared Prosperity

In today's marriages, stability requires teamwork. Financial independence, mutual decision-making, and equal sharing of responsibilities have redefined the first vow. A modern couple might reframe the vow as:

"Together, we will build a secure and emotionally nourishing life, balancing career, finances, family, and love."

Financial Nourishment: The Practical Foundation

Money is one of the leading causes of marital conflict. Studies show that financial disagreements predict divorce more strongly than fights about other issues. Couples who align on money early often experience greater harmony.

💡 **Case Study – The Budget Battle:** Radhika and Aman, both working professionals, often fought over finances. She valued experiences—travel, dining out—

while he prioritized savings. Their constant arguments left them drained. Finally, they sat down and created a **three-tier plan**:

- **Short-term goals:** Rent, groceries, bills.
- **Medium-term goals:** A vacation and buying a car.
- **Long-term goals:** Retirement savings and children's education.

This shift—from "me vs. you" to "us vs. the problem"—replaced conflict with teamwork.

☞ **Lesson:** The vow of nourishment is fulfilled not by earning more, but by aligning values around money.

Emotional Nourishment: Feeding the Heart

Stability is not only about what's on the plate but also about what's in the heart. Emotional starvation—feeling unseen, unheard, or unsupported—can erode a marriage faster than financial scarcity.

✨ **Story – Evening Tea Ritual:** Meena, a schoolteacher, returned home exhausted daily. Her husband, Sameer, noticed her silence but didn't know how to help. One evening, he suggested a ritual: during tea, they'd each share "one good thing" and "one hard thing" from the day. Over time, this small practice deepened their intimacy. Meena later said, *"Those 15 minutes nourished me more than any meal."*

Spiritual Nourishment: Anchoring the Soul

Spiritual stability doesn't necessarily mean religion—it could mean mindfulness, shared values, or practices that ground the couple.

❢ **Example:** An interfaith couple in Delhi chose meditation as their shared practice. Every morning, they sat in silence for 10 minutes. This practice became their anchor—reminding them that beneath cultural differences, they shared a soul connection.

Challenges in Modern Relationships

- **Dual-Career Burnout:** Both partners juggle demanding jobs, leaving little energy for family life.
- **Unequal Household Division:** Old stereotypes linger, causing resentment if one partner bears more.
- **Financial Pressure:** Rising costs, debt, and lifestyle comparisons strain marriages.
- **Work-Life Imbalance:** Technology blurs work boundaries, stealing time meant for family.

Reflection Questions

1. Do we openly share our financial goals and struggles, or avoid money talks?
2. How do we currently nourish each other emotionally? What can we add?
3. What does "prosperity" mean to us—only money, or also joy, peace, and balance?
4. Which daily rituals make us feel stable and connected?

Write your reflections below.

Couple's Exercises

1. **The Prosperity Jar:** Take a jar labeled *Our Prosperity Jar*. Every week, drop in one note of something you did that nourished your relationship (a kind word, cooking together, saving for a goal). At year's end, open it together.

2. **Financial Vision Board:** Create a board with images of your shared financial goals—home, travel, children's education. Place it somewhere visible. Seeing goals daily reduces conflict and increases motivation.

3. **Emotional Check-Ins:** Dedicate 10 minutes daily: each partner shares "one good thing, one tough thing, one hope for tomorrow."

4. **Shared Spiritual Practice:** Choose one grounding ritual—gratitude journaling, lighting a diya, meditation, or prayer. Practicing together strengthens inner stability.

Illustrative Story – The Empty Pantry

In a small town, a newly married couple often faced an empty pantry. They cooked simple meals—rice with salt, lentils stretched over days. Yet, they made cooking together joyful, sometimes inviting neighbors to share what little they had. Years later, after becoming financially stable, they often recalled those days as their happiest.

☞ **Lesson:** Nourishment is never about abundance; it is about attitude. Even in scarcity, couples can feel wealthy when they share laughter, kindness, and hope.

Psychological Insight: Maslow's Hierarchy in Marriage

Maslow's pyramid begins with basic needs—food, shelter, safety. Without these, higher needs like love and self-actualization suffer. The first vow reminds couples to secure the base together. Once stability is established, they can climb toward emotional intimacy, growth, and legacy.

Closing Thought

The first vow is the soil in which the marriage grows. Without nourishment, a relationship withers. With it, love blossoms—transforming shared meals into communion, financial planning into partnership, and daily rituals into sacred acts.

Marriage thrives when partners ask not only *"What can I receive?"* but *"What can I give to nourish us?"* Stability is not built overnight—it is cultivated, moment by moment, meal by meal, conversation by conversation.

Chapter - 5

The Second Vow: Emotional and Spiritual Support

If the first vow lays the foundation of nourishment, the second vow builds the heart of marriage: **emotional and spiritual support.** Food and shelter sustain the body, but empathy, understanding, and encouragement sustain the soul.

The couple promises:

- **The groom:** *"I will stand by you, provide emotional support, and encourage your spiritual growth."*
- **The bride:** *"I will be your companion, offering love, care, and understanding as we walk this path together."*

At its core, this vow is about becoming each other's **anchor during hardship** and **inspiration during calm.**

Why Emotional Support Matters

Psychologists say one of the greatest predictors of marital satisfaction is not wealth or attraction but the feeling of being **emotionally understood.** When couples feel heard, valued, and supported, they develop resilience against life's storms.

On the other hand, emotional neglect—when one partner feels invisible or dismissed—often becomes the silent crack that leads to separation.

Modern-Day Challenges to Emotional Connection

1. **Digital Distraction:** Phones and screens rob couples of presence.
2. **Work Pressure:** Exhaustion leaves little room for deep conversations.
3. **Mental Health Issues:** Depression, anxiety, and burnout strain intimacy.
4. **Extended Family Pressures:** Cultural expectations can weaken emotional closeness.
5. **Individual vs. Shared Goals:** One partner's ambitions may leave the other feeling side lined.

Stories of Emotional Support

💡 **The Phone Wall:** Ritu often sat beside her husband, Anil, who spent evenings scrolling social media. She longed for conversation but felt invisible. One evening she finally said, *"I don't need your presence in the room, I need your presence with me."* Anil was shocked—he thought being home was enough. They made a rule: no phones at dinner. That one small decision rebuilt connection.

✨ **Standing Through Mental Health Struggles:** After losing his job, Karan slipped into depression. His wife, Asha, initially felt helpless and frustrated. But instead of withdrawing, she encouraged him to seek therapy and even joined him at his first session. Later, Karan said, *"Her presence was my medicine."* This is the second vow in action: not solving problems, but staying present through them.

✿ **The Silent Bridge:** In a village, an elderly couple known for their long marriage shared their secret: *"When angry, we built a bridge of silence."* Instead of shouting, they sat quietly side by side until calm returned. Then they spoke kindly. Their silence was not withdrawal but a reminder: *"Our bond is stronger than this moment of anger."*

Spiritual Support: Beyond Religion

Spiritual support doesn't always mean prayer—it can be shared mindfulness, reflection, or simply reminding each other of values.

💡 **Example:** A young couple in Pune began a gratitude ritual. Each night, they told each other one thing they appreciated that day. Within months, arguments reduced, and closeness increased. Gratitude became their "spiritual glue."

Psychological Insights

- **Attachment Theory:** Securely attached couples offer comfort during distress. Anxious or avoidant patterns often create misunderstandings.
- **Active Listening:** True listening is hearing emotions, not just words. Couples who practice this feel more validated.
- **Co-regulation:** Partners can calm each other's stress through touch, presence, and empathy.

Reflection Questions

1. Do I listen with empathy, or only to reply?
2. How often do I celebrate my partner's wins?
3. What rituals do we have for emotional or spiritual connection?
4. When my partner is struggling, do I offer judgment, advice, or presence?

Write your reflections below.

Couple's Exercises

1. **Daily Emotional Check-In:** Ask each other three questions:
    - What was the best part of your day?
    - What was the hardest part?
    - How can I support you tomorrow?
2. **Technology-Free Hour:** Dedicate one hour daily (or a few times weekly) for device-free connection—cooking, walking, or just talking.
3. **Celebrate Small Wins:** Acknowledge even small achievements—a finished report, a new recipe, or completing a workout. Recognition builds emotional closeness.
4. **Shared Spiritual Practice:** Choose one ritual—prayer, meditation, gratitude journaling, or yoga. Practicing together deepens intimacy.

Mini-Stories of Emotional and Spiritual Support

✨ **The Meditation Bench:** An elderly couple in Chennai sat every evening on a garden bench, meditating for 15 minutes together. This ritual, small yet sacred, became their emotional anchor for decades.

✿ **The Listening Jar:** A couple in Mumbai created a "listening jar." They wrote topics or emotions on slips of paper. Each week, they picked one and discussed it deeply. What began as a playful exercise became their lifeline for communication.

Practical Tips for Strengthening Support

- Use "I feel" instead of "You never."
- Schedule weekly "heart talks" where you discuss emotions, not logistics.
- Offer physical presence—hug, hold hands, or sit nearby. Touch often communicates support better than words.
- Encourage personal growth—celebrate your partner's hobbies and passions.

Commitment Exercise

Together, write a support statement in your own words. For example:

"We commit to listening deeply, supporting each other's growth, and being present even in silence or struggle."

Place it where you can see it often.

Closing Thought

The second vow reminds us that marriage is not just about companionship but about being a safe space for each other. Emotional and spiritual support transforms a house into a home, and two individuals into soul partners.

Storms will come—job losses, illnesses, misunderstandings—but if couples honor this vow, they discover that love is not the absence of struggle, but the promise of presence.

Chapter - 6

The Third Vow: Commitment to Self-Discipline and Action

The first vow secures nourishment, the second vow builds emotional support, and the third vow teaches couples the discipline of action. Love without responsibility remains a dream; responsibility without action becomes frustration. The third vow reminds couples that **marriage thrives not on promises spoken once, but on actions repeated daily.**

In the sacred fire ritual, the couple pledges:

"Together, we will live with self-discipline, work diligently, and act with responsibility. We will walk the path of action, not excuses."

This vow is about **showing up—consistently, intentionally, and with integrity.**

Why Action Matters in Marriage

Every relationship begins with emotion but is sustained by habits. A spouse may feel love but if that love is never expressed—in words, gestures, or efforts—it withers.

- Promises are remembered; actions are trusted.
- Small daily efforts—sharing chores, remembering dates, listening without distraction—are the "bricks" of a strong marriage.
- Self-discipline ensures couples don't act only when convenient but even when difficult.

Common Excuses Couples Make

- "I don't have time."
- "This is just how I am."
- "I'll do it tomorrow."
- "Why should I start? Let them make the effort."

❢ **Insight:** Excuses feel safe but silently damage connection. Over time, partners stop relying on each other when words never match actions.

Real-Life Stories of Action

✨ **Neha's Writing Journey:** Neha dreamed of writing a book for years but procrastinated. Her husband encouraged her to dedicate just 30 minutes daily. He took over chores during that time. Two years later, her manuscript was complete. Neha said, *"His consistency* *in supporting me was the discipline I needed to stay committed."*

✿ **Arjun's Career Pivot:** Arjun wanted to change industries but avoided taking action, citing "no time." His wife suggested the "15-minute rule." Every evening, he studied for 15 minutes. Within six months, he had the skills for a new role. Their marriage grew stronger because they learned to fight excuses together.

❢ **The Couple Who Chose Health:** Ravi and Kavita constantly postponed exercise, blaming work stress. After a health scare, they made a pact: walk 20 minutes daily, no matter what. Over time, the walks became not only exercise but also their "talk time." They realized self-discipline gave them both health and intimacy.

Psychological Insights

- **The Habit Loop:** Cue → Routine → Reward. Couples who create shared habits (like walks, gratitude, or financial planning) build trust.
- **Consistency > Intensity:** Research shows small, consistent actions are more effective than occasional grand gestures.
- **Growth Mindset:** Viewing failures as feedback encourages couples to keep improving instead of quitting.

Reflection Questions

1. In what areas of our marriage do we rely on excuses?
2. What small, consistent action would make our relationship stronger?
3. Do we celebrate each other's efforts, or only results?
4. What rituals of discipline can we create together?

Write your reflections below.

Couple's Exercises

1. **Excuse Audit:** Each partner lists their top 3 excuses (e.g., "too tired," "no time"). Discuss the fear or belief behind each excuse.

2. **The Two-Minute Rule:** Choose one task (talking, walking, journaling). Commit to just 2 minutes daily. Often, momentum makes it longer.

3. **Action Contract:** Write one responsibility you'll take consistently (e.g., paying bills on time, planning date nights, checking in emotionally). Sign it together as a "third vow contract."

4. **Weekly Progress Check-In:** Every Sunday, spend 10 minutes asking: "What action this week strengthened our marriage? What can we do better next week?"

Mindset Shifts

- From *"I'll do it when I feel like it"* → *"I'll do it because I value us."*
- From *"I failed once, so I can't"* → *"Each attempt is practice."*
- From *"Big change is overwhelming"* → *"Small steps create momentum."*

Mini-Stories of Discipline

✨ **The Morning Gratitude Ritual:** A couple began each day by sharing one gratitude. At first it felt forced, but after weeks, it became their favorite ritual. Years later, they credit this tiny act with keeping positivity alive.

❁ **The Accountability Pact:** Two partners struggling with savings created a pact: every unnecessary purchase had to be approved by both. What began as financial discipline became a symbol of teamwork.

Commitment Exercise

Write your Third Vow in your own words. For example:

"We commit to consistent action, to replacing excuses with effort, and to showing our love through daily responsibility."

Read it aloud together each morning for one week.

Closing Thought

The third vow teaches that love is not passive—it is a verb. A marriage thrives when partners act, not when they wait. Small, consistent actions—washing dishes, listening deeply, planning for the future—become sacred when done with intention.

Discipline is not about rigidity; it is about reliability. When two people can trust that the other will show up—even in small ways—their love becomes not just an emotion but a legacy of action.

Chapter – 7

The Fourth Vow: Resilience and Handling Setbacks

No life is free from challenges. Careers falter, health declines, dreams fail, and relationships encounter storms. The **fourth vow of marriage** asks couples to walk through hardship with courage and resilience. It reminds us that setbacks are not the end of love but an invitation to grow stronger together.

In the traditional ritual, the couple pledges:

"We will face difficulties together with courage. We will recover from setbacks with strength and learn from every challenge."

This vow is about resilience—not the absence of struggle, but the art of bouncing back.

Why Resilience Matters in Marriage

Research shows resilient couples are not those who avoid problems but those who adapt. They view challenges as temporary, solvable, and even opportunities for growth.

- **Every couple faces storms.** It's not "if" but "when."
- **Resilience creates trust.** Knowing your partner will stay through hardship deepens love.
- **Setbacks can transform.** Many couples report feeling closer after surviving difficulties.

Real-Life Stories of Resilience

✨ **Anjali's Business Failure:** At 28, Anjali launched a clothing brand. Six months later, it collapsed due to financial missteps. She felt crushed. Her husband reminded her, *"This failure doesn't define you; it teaches us."* With his encouragement, she analyzed mistakes, sought mentorship, and started again. Within two years, her second venture thrived. She later said, *"My resilience wasn't mine alone—it was ours."*

✿ **Rahul's Career Pivot:** When Rahul lost his job unexpectedly, panic set in. His wife, Kavita, sat with him and together they created a "bounce-back plan"—he would learn new skills while she took extra shifts. Within six months, Rahul found a better job. Later he admitted, *"Her belief in me was my confidence when I had none."*

❢ **Suresh and Anjali at 60:** This couple faced multiple storms—debt, illnesses, and family disputes. Yet, instead of blaming, they reframed each setback as a shared lesson. Today, their children say, *"Our parents never hid struggles from us. They showed us how to fight together, not alone."*

Challenges That Test Resilience

1. **Financial Crisis:** Job losses, debt, or unexpected expenses.
2. **Health Issues:** Chronic illness, infertility, or sudden accidents.
3. **Family Conflicts:** Interference from relatives, parenting struggles.
4. **Unmet Expectations:** Dreams that don't align or goals that collapse.
5. **Societal Pressures:** Comparisons with peers or cultural stigmas.

Psychological Insights

- **Post-Traumatic Growth:** Couples often emerge stronger after surviving crises.
- **Reframing:** Shifting language from "This is the end" to "This is a lesson" changes outlook.
- **Emotional Recovery:** Resilience requires processing emotions—denial or suppression weakens it.

- **Adaptability:** The ability to pivot together builds survival strength.

Reflection Questions

1. How do we usually react during setbacks—panic, blame, or problem-solving?
2. Do we process pain together, or withdraw into silence?
3. What past challenges have actually brought us closer?
4. What personal habits (gratitude, optimism, discipline) strengthen my resilience?

Write your reflections below.

Couple's Exercises

1. **Setback Journal:** Write about your last setback: What happened? What did you learn? How did you grow? Share entries with each other.
2. **Micro-Recovery Actions:** After a failure, choose 1–3 small steps to regain momentum (sending one job application, making one doctor's appointment, cooking one meal together).
3. **Emotional Reset Ritual:** Create a ritual to release stress—walks, journaling, or lighting a candle. Use it whenever life feels overwhelming.
4. **Resilience Visualization:** Close your eyes and picture yourself overcoming a current challenge. Share your vision with your partner.

Mini-Stories of Resilience

✨ **Simran's Exam Struggles:** Simran failed her competitive exams twice. Instead of shaming her, her husband helped her structure study plans and celebrated small wins. On her third attempt, she succeeded. She said, *"His patience was the rope that pulled me from despair."*

✿ **Vikram's Startup Journey:** Vikram's first two startups collapsed. By the third attempt, his wife's encouragement—"We are building resilience, not just businesses"—kept him going. Today, they credit failures for their success.

Mindset Shifts

- From *"I failed, so I'm a failure"* → *"I failed, but I'm learning."*
- From *"Setbacks destroy us"* → *"Setbacks strengthen us."*
- From *"We need perfect conditions"* → *"We adapt to conditions as they come."*

Commitment Exercise

Write your own Fourth Vow together. Example:

"We commit to courage in storms, patience in trials, and learning in failures. We will not let setbacks define us but will use them to grow stronger."

Read this aloud whenever challenges feel overwhelming.

Closing Thought

The fourth vow teaches that love is not fragile. Hardships do not break couples—they reveal their strength. Resilient marriages are not perfect but persistent. They bend, but they don't break.

When partners stand together, even the fiercest storm becomes survivable. The question is never "Will storms come?" but "Will we hold each other through them?"

If the answer is yes, then resilience becomes not only a vow but a lived reality—a love tested, refined, and unshakable.

Chapter – 8

The Fifth Vow: Purposeful Living and Legacy

The first four vows prepare the couple with nourishment, support, discipline, and resilience. The **fifth vow** elevates marriage to a higher plane—it is about **living with purpose and leaving behind a legacy.**

In the sacred fire ceremony, the couple pledges:

"We will walk together to uphold our duties toward family, society, and the greater good. We will strive to live meaningfully and leave behind a legacy of values, love, and contribution."

Marriage, then, is not only about two people—it is about creating something that outlasts them.

The Meaning of Purpose in Marriage

Purpose is the compass that guides couples when daily routines feel repetitive. It gives meaning to struggles and inspiration to rise each morning.

- Without purpose, life feels like survival.
- With purpose, even small tasks feel sacred.

For some, purpose may be raising children with strong values. For others, it may be serving community, building a business, or creating art together. Every couple has a unique definition of legacy.

Real-Life Stories of Legacy

✨ **Ravi and Lata – Teaching Beyond Classrooms:** Both schoolteachers, Ravi and Lata believed their purpose extended beyond their own family. Together, they started weekend classes for underprivileged children. Their children grew up watching this, absorbing compassion as a way of life. Today, their legacy is not just their biological children but dozens of students who call them mentors.

✿ **Farhan and Noor – Parenting with Purpose:** Farhan and Noor decided early that their legacy would be raising conscious children. Instead of just focusing on grades, they emphasized empathy, storytelling, and volunteering. Today, their teenage daughter leads environmental campaigns in school. Their legacy is a child who carries forward their values.

❢ **The Elderly Couple in Varanasi:** After retirement, an elderly couple in Varanasi began planting trees along the riverbanks. In 20 years, they had planted more than 10,000 trees. They often said, *"Our children will inherit wealth from us. But society should inherit shade and breath."*

Purpose Beyond Parenthood

While many view legacy as raising children, purpose extends further:

- Creating businesses that serve people.
- Supporting social causes.
- Writing books, music, or art that inspire.
- Mentoring others.
- Living as role models of compassion, courage, and faithfulness.

☞ **Insight:** Not every couple may have children. But every couple can leave a legacy through the lives they touch.

Challenges to Purposeful Living

1. **Routine Fatigue:** Daily chores can overshadow long-term vision.
2. **Materialism:** Focusing only on money and possessions often leaves couples unfulfilled.
3. **Comparison:** Measuring legacy against others creates anxiety.

4. **Lack of Clarity:** Many couples never discuss what "purpose" means for them.

Psychological Insights

- **Logotherapy (Viktor Frankl):** Humans can survive any suffering if they find meaning in it. Couples too can thrive if they unite under shared meaning.
- **Generativity (Erik Erikson):** In adulthood, people seek to create or nurture things that will outlast them—this is the essence of the fifth vow.
- **Positive Psychology:** A life of contribution creates deeper happiness than a life of consumption.

Reflection Questions

1. What do we want our family and friends to remember us for?
2. What values do we want to pass on to the next generation?
3. Are we living only for comfort, or also for contribution?
4. How do we want our marriage to impact society?

Write your reflections below.

Couple's Exercises

1. **Legacy Letter:** Write a letter together imagining your 50th wedding anniversary. What do you want your children, community, or friends to say about you?

2. **Purpose Map:** Create a chart with three circles: *Family, Career, Society.* Write down contributions you'd like to make in each. Discuss how to take the first step.

3. **Value Jar:** Write core values (honesty, compassion, courage, etc.) on slips of paper. Each week, pick one and consciously practice it as a couple.

4. **Annual Service Tradition:** Decide on one activity every year that contributes beyond your family—charity, volunteering, mentorship, or community service.

Mini-Stories of Purpose

✨ **The Café of Kindness:** A couple in Bengaluru opened a small café where customers could pre-pay meals for the homeless. Over time, their café became known as a place of generosity. Their children learned that business can also be service.

✿ **The Journal Legacy:** One couple decided to keep a family journal—writing stories, struggles, and wisdom. Years later, their grandchildren read it as a treasure of life lessons. Their legacy was not wealth, but wisdom.

Commitment Exercise

Together, write your Fifth Vow in your own words. Example:

"We commit to live with purpose, to serve beyond ourselves, and to leave behind a legacy of love, kindness, and contribution."

Place it where you can see it, so daily life aligns with your higher purpose.

Closing Thought

The fifth vow transforms marriage from partnership to purpose. It reminds us that life is not only about paying bills or celebrating anniversaries but about creating ripples that outlast us.

A legacy is not measured in monuments but in memories—how people felt in our presence, how our children live our values, how society is kinder because we walked together.

When couples align around purpose, they discover that their love is not just for each other but for the world.

Chapter – 9

The Sixth Vow: Nurturing Family and Children

Marriage is not only about two individuals—it is about weaving a network of relationships that extends across generations. The **sixth vow of marriage** emphasizes the couple's responsibility to nurture family bonds, raise children with values, and care for elders.

In the sacred wedding ritual, the couple pledges:

"We will share the responsibility of raising children, guiding them with love and wisdom. We will honor our family, respect our elders, and strengthen the lineage we belong to."

This vow recognizes that love matures when it expands—when it moves from the couple to children, from the household to community, from the present to the future.

Parenthood as a Sacred Responsibility

Raising children is not just about feeding and educating them—it is about shaping their values, character, and worldview. A child absorbs not what parents preach but what they live.

❢ **Insight:** Children raised in households where love, respect, and cooperation are modeled grow into adults who carry those values into society.

Real-Life Stories of Family Nurturing

✨ **Meera and Sanjay – Balancing Work and Parenthood:** Both IT professionals, they struggled to balance work with parenting. Instead of one partner carrying the full load, they created a schedule: Sanjay handled mornings, Meera evenings. They also introduced a "no-work family hour" daily. Their daughter grew up saying, *"My parents always had time for me."*

✿ **A Couple Without Children:** Raj and Nandini were unable to have children. At first, they felt incomplete. But with time, they redefined the sixth vow as nurturing their extended family. They mentored nieces and nephews, supported neighbors' kids in studies, and funded scholarships. Years later, dozens of young adults called them role models.

☞ **Lesson:** Nurturing is not limited to biological children—it is about creating safe spaces for growth.

❢ **An Elderly Couple Caring for Parents:** Vikram and Priya chose to live with Vikram's aging parents, despite the challenges. They divided responsibilities and ensured dignity for elders. Their children grew up witnessing this, learning compassion by example.

Challenges in Nurturing Family

1. **Work-Life Imbalance:** Busy schedules limit family time.
2. **Generational Gaps:** Different values between parents, children, and elders cause conflict.
3. **Cultural Shifts:** Traditional joint families are giving way to nuclear setups.
4. **Parenting Pressure:** Academic and social expectations overwhelm both parents and kids.
5. **Marriages Without Children:** Couples may feel judged by society, leading to emotional pain.

Psychological Insights

- **Family Systems Theory (Bowen):** A family is an emotional unit; changes in one member affect all. Healthy families balance individuality with togetherness.
- **Attachment Theory:** Secure parent-child bonds predict confidence, empathy, and resilience in children.
- **Intergenerational Transmission:** Values and behaviors pass down generations, consciously or unconsciously.

Reflection Questions

1. How do we divide parenting responsibilities—fairly or traditionally?
2. What values are we consciously modeling for children or younger family members?
3. Do we balance family obligations with our couple's intimacy?
4. How do we want our family to remember us as parents, children, or caregivers?

Write your reflections below.

Couple's Exercises

1. **Family Vision Statement:** Together, write 5 core values you want your family to embody (e.g., honesty, kindness, courage). Display it at home.
2. **Weekly Family Ritual:** Create one ritual everyone looks forward to—Sunday lunch, Friday movie night, or daily gratitude circle.
3. **Storytelling Tradition:** Share family stories with children about courage, resilience, or kindness. Stories carry values better than lectures.
4. **Elder Care Plan:** Discuss how to support aging parents—financially, emotionally, and physically—without resentment or burnout.

Mini-Stories of Family Nurturing

✨ **The Dinner Table Rule:** One couple made a strict rule: no devices at dinner. This became their sacred bonding time where children shared stories. Years later, their grown children remembered dinner conversations as the "heart of family life."

🌼 **The Adopted Family:** A couple who couldn't conceive adopted two children. They said, *"Blood doesn't define family—love does."* Their nurturing created a legacy as powerful as any lineage.

Mindset Shifts

- From *"Family is a burden"* → *"Family is our anchor."*
- From *"Children must achieve"* → *"Children must flourish."*
- From *"We don't have children, so we lack legacy"* → *"We can nurture in many ways."*

Commitment Exercise

Write your own Sixth Vow. Example:

"We commit to nurturing family bonds, raising children or guiding the young with wisdom, and honoring elders with love and dignity."

Read it aloud together when making important family decisions.

Closing Thought

The sixth vow expands love outward. It reminds us that marriage is not an island but a bridge between generations. By nurturing children, guiding the young, and caring for elders, couples transform their marriage into a legacy of values.

Family is not always easy—it requires patience, compromise, and sacrifice. Yet, the joy of seeing children grow, of honoring parents, and of belonging to a lineage makes the effort worthwhile.

In the end, nurturing family is not about perfection but about presence—the willingness to show up with love, again and again.

Chapter - 10

The Seventh Vow: Lifelong Companionship & Friendship

The seven vows culminate in the most tender and profound promise—the vow of **lifelong companionship and friendship.**

In the sacred fire ritual, the couple pledges:

"We will remain companions for life, walking together in love, loyalty, and friendship. We will share joys and sorrows, dreams and fears, until our final breath."

This vow is the soul of marriage. Love may ignite the bond, but friendship sustains it.

Friendship: The Heart of Marriage

Friendship is built on **acceptance, laughter, trust, and shared moments.** When spouses see each other not just as partners but as friends, the marriage becomes a safe space—a refuge in a world that can be demanding.

- Lovers admire each other.
- Partners share responsibilities.
- Friends delight in each other.

☞ **Insight:** A marriage rooted in friendship weathers storms because companionship makes even hardships lighter.

Real-Life Stories of Friendship in Marriage

✨ **Ramesh and Kavita – Laughter as Medicine:** Ramesh was known for his humor, and Kavita adored it. Even during financial struggles, he cracked jokes to lighten her stress. Decades later, their children recall, *"Our parents taught us that laughter is not ignoring problems but surviving them together."*

✿ **The Bedtime Ritual:** One couple, married 25 years, made it a rule to never sleep without saying, *"I love you."* Even after arguments, the ritual softened egos. They explained, *"We may not always agree, but we always belong."*

❢ **An Elderly Couple Walking Together:** In a small town, an elderly pair walked hand in hand every evening. A child once asked them, *"Why do you still walk together?"* The husband smiled, *"Because even* *after 50 years, I don't want to miss her stories."* Their companionship was not about grand gestures but daily presence.

Challenges to Companionship

1. **Routine Fatigue:** Friendship fades when couples stop playing, laughing, or sharing joys.
2. **Unresolved Conflicts:** Lingering bitterness erodes companionship.
3. **Overemphasis on Roles:** Seeing each other only as "parent," "provider," or "homemaker" reduces friendship.
4. **Growing Apart:** Without shared activities, partners may drift into parallel lives.

Psychological Insights

- **Gottman's Research:** The strongest predictor of marital happiness is friendship—shared jokes, emotional support, and admiration.
- **Companionship vs. Codependency:** True companionship supports individuality while celebrating togetherness.
- **Play Therapy for Adults:** Play (games, adventures, humor) restores intimacy and reduces stress.

Reflection Questions

1. Do we treat each other as friends, or only as roles (parent, spouse, breadwinner)?
2. What activities bring us joy together? Do we still make time for them?
3. Do we share secrets, dreams, and laughter as friends do?
4. How do we nurture friendship when routine takes over?

Write your reflections below.

Couple's Exercises

1. **Friendship Date:** Plan a date as if you are best friends—not spouses. Do something fun, silly, or adventurous.

2. **Memory Box:** Create a box of shared memories—photos, letters, tokens. Open it together once a year to relive friendship.

3. **Dream Sharing:** Once a week, share one dream or goal (personal or professional). Encourage and support it like a best friend would.

4. **The Compliment Game:** Each night, say one genuine compliment to your partner. Over time, admiration becomes habit.

Mini-Stories of Friendship

✨ **The Rain Walk:** A young couple once fought bitterly, but during a sudden downpour, they laughed and danced in the rain. Years later, they still said, *"That rain taught us that joy is always possible if we choose it."*

✿ **Travel Partners:** One couple decided their marriage would be measured in journeys, not possessions. Every year, they traveled somewhere new, even if on a small budget. Their friendship grew through shared adventures.

Mindset Shifts

- From *"Marriage is duty"* → *"Marriage is friendship."*
- From *"We must be serious adults"* → *"We can keep playing together."*
- From *"Love fades with time"* → *"Friendship deepens with time."*

Commitment Exercise

Write your own Seventh Vow. Example:

"We commit to lifelong companionship, to laughter and loyalty, to walking as friends until the end of our journey."

Frame it, or place it in your bedroom as a reminder.

Closing Thought

The seventh vow is not the end of the marriage journey—it is the beginning of a lifelong friendship. Lovers may change with time, parents may age, roles may shift—but true friends remain constant.

Marriage thrives when couples continue to share jokes, adventures, secrets, and dreams as they did in the early days. Companionship is not found once; it is chosen daily.

When two people promise not only to love but also to be each other's best friend, their marriage becomes more than a bond—it becomes a lifelong celebration.

Chapter – 11

Challenges to the Seven Vows in Modern Marriages

The seven vows offer timeless wisdom, but living them in today's fast-paced, ever-changing world requires new strength. Couples are no longer bound only by tradition—they face pressures from careers, technology, individual ambitions, and evolving cultural values.

This chapter explores the **modern challenges to each vow** and how couples can adapt without losing the essence of commitment.

Challenge to the First Vow – Nourishment and Stability

- **Modern Pressure:** Dual careers, financial uncertainty, inflation, and lifestyle comparisons.
- **Impact:** Couples may argue about money, leading to resentment. Some prioritize material possessions over emotional nourishment.
- **Example:** A young couple constantly fought because one wanted to save aggressively while the other wanted to enjoy experiences like travel.

☞ **Adaptation:** Stability today is not about one partner providing—it's about **financial teamwork, open discussions, and emotional nourishment alongside material comfort.**

Challenge to the Second Vow – Emotional and Spiritual Support

- **Modern Pressure:** Overuse of technology and social media creates emotional distance.
- **Impact:** Partners may spend more time on screens than with each other, leading to feelings of neglect.
- **Example:** Riya felt lonelier sitting beside her husband while he scrolled Instagram than when he was at work.

☞ **Adaptation:** Couples must consciously carve out **"sacred time"** for conversations, rituals, and presence without digital interference.

Challenge to the Third Vow – Self-Discipline and Action

- **Modern Pressure:** Busyness and distractions lead to procrastination and broken promises.
- **Impact:** Excuses like "no time" or "too tired" erode trust when words don't match actions.
- **Example:** A husband promised weekly date nights but canceled often for work. Over time, his wife stopped expecting effort.

☞ **Adaptation:** The vow of action today means **small, consistent efforts matter more than rare grand gestures.**

Challenge to the Fourth Vow – Resilience and Handling Setbacks

- **Modern Pressure:** The culture of instant gratification makes people less tolerant of difficulties.

- **Impact:** Instead of working through setbacks, some couples see separation as the first solution.

- **Example:** After financial loss, a couple grew distant instead of supporting each other. Blame replaced resilience.

☞ **Adaptation:** Couples need to **reframe setbacks as shared battles** and learn skills like problem-solving, therapy, and emotional regulation.

Challenge to the Fifth Vow – Purposeful Living and Legacy

- **Modern Pressure:** Materialism and the "rat race" overshadow higher purpose.

- **Impact:** Couples may focus on possessions instead of values, leaving children without guidance on meaning.

- **Example:** Parents gifted their child expensive gadgets but had no time to instill empathy or resilience.

☞ **Adaptation:** Purpose today requires **intentional discussions about values, contributions, and legacy beyond wealth.**

Challenge to the Sixth Vow – Nurturing Family and Children

- **Modern Pressure:** Parenting competition (academic scores, extra curriculars, social image).
- **Impact:** Children may feel pressured, and parents may exhaust themselves. Eldercare also adds stress in nuclear families.
- **Example:** A couple pushed their child into endless coaching classes, leaving no space for play or family connection.

☞ **Adaptation:** Couples must **balance ambition with emotional care** and remember that nurturing is more than achievement.

Challenge to the Seventh Vow – Lifelong Companionship

- **Modern Pressure:** High divorce rates, casual relationships, and constant comparison through social media.
- **Impact:** Some partners see marriage as replaceable when difficulties arise.
- **Example:** Anushka compared her husband to "Instagram husbands" who posted grand gestures, leading to dissatisfaction.

☞ **Adaptation:** True companionship requires **valuing daily presence, humor, and loyalty over online perfection.**

Wider Social Challenges

1. **Cultural Shifts:** From joint to nuclear families, weakening traditional support systems.
2. **Global Mobility:** Long-distance marriages due to jobs abroad.
3. **Individualism:** "Me first" culture clashes with "we first" of marriage.
4. **Mental Health Struggles:** Anxiety, depression, and stress can strain vows if left unaddressed.

Psychological Insights

- **Expectation Gap:** Research shows unmet expectations—often shaped by movies or social media—fuel disappointment.
- **Comparison Trap:** Constant comparison erodes gratitude.
- **Emotional Intelligence:** Couples with higher EQ handle challenges more successfully.

Reflection Questions

1. Which vow do we find hardest to live in today's lifestyle?
2. Do external pressures (social media, family, career) dictate our marriage more than our own values?
3. What modern habits harm our companionship, and how can we replace them?

Write your reflections below.

Couple's Exercises

1. **Digital Detox Hour:** Dedicate one hour daily as tech-free time for conversations or shared activities.
2. **Vows Check-In:** Once a month, reflect: Which vow are we honoring well? Which needs attention?
3. **Gratitude Swap:** Each partner writes one gratitude for the other daily. Over time, it rebuilds admiration.
4. **Couple's Therapy/Coaching:** Normalize seeking help—modern challenges require modern tools.

Closing Thought

The seven vows were created centuries ago, yet their spirit remains timeless. The real challenge lies not in their relevance but in their application amidst today's distractions and pressures.

A marriage does not fail because challenges arise—it falters when couples stop adapting. When partners recognize the obstacles of modern life and still choose to honor their vows, they prove that love is not bound by time or tradition—it is an ever-renewing choice.

Chapter – 12

Practical Ways to Renew and Revisit the Vows in Modern Life

The seven vows are not meant to be remembered only on the wedding day—they are living promises, meant to be revisited, renewed, and reinterpreted throughout life.

In modern marriages, renewal is essential. Just as a plant needs water regularly, a relationship thrives when partners intentionally nurture it. This chapter offers practical ways couples can breathe fresh life into their vows at different stages of marriage.

Why Renewal Matters

- **Memories Fade:** Over time, couples may forget the sacred promises.
- **Life Changes:** New challenges—parenthood, career shifts, aging parents—demand new interpretations of vows.
- **Love Evolves:** Renewal acknowledges that love is not static but dynamic.

☞ **Insight:** Vows are not words etched in stone—they are choices written daily in actions.

Daily Practices to Revisit the Vows

1. **Morning Gratitude Ritual:** Each morning, share one thing you are grateful for in your partner. Nourishes the first vow of stability.

2. **Evening Check-In:** Spend 10 minutes nightly asking: "How was your day? How can I support you tomorrow?" Keeps the second vow alive.

3. **Shared Discipline Calendar:** Track one daily discipline together (exercise, prayer, or journaling). Builds the third vow of action.

4. **Weekly Family Meeting:** Discuss family goals, finances, and challenges. Strengthens the sixth vow of nurturing family.

5. **Companionship Time:** Dedicate 20 minutes daily to companionship—walk, tea, or humor. Keeps the seventh vow vibrant.

Anniversary Renewal Rituals

- **Vows Revisited Ceremony:** On anniversaries, light a candle or stand by a small fire, and re-speak the vows in your own words.
- **Letter to Each Other:** Write letters annually reflecting how you honored the vows that year. Exchange them as gifts.
- **Symbolic Rituals:** Plant a tree (legacy), exchange flowers (acceptance), or take seven steps together (renewal).

Seasonal or Yearly Practices

1. **Quarterly Retreat:** Take a short trip together to reflect on progress, setbacks, and dreams.
2. **Vision Board Update:** Refresh your family vision board yearly to align with new goals.
3. **Legacy Reflection:** On birthdays or anniversaries, ask: "What legacy are we building this year?"

Conflict-Resolution Through Vows

When arguments arise, revisit the vows:

- **Dispute over finances?** Return to the first vow—nourishment means teamwork.
- **Emotional neglect?** Recall the second vow—support requires presence.

- **Procrastination?** Remember the third vow—discipline sustains love.
- **Blame during hardship?** Lean on the fourth vow—resilience means "we" not "me."
- **Feeling purposeless?** Revisit the fifth vow—purpose is our shared compass.
- **Parenting stress?** Return to the sixth vow—nurturing, not competing.
- **Drifting apart?** Honor the seventh vow—friendship is the core of marriage.

☞ **Exercise:** During conflicts, pause and ask: *"Which vow are we forgetting right now?"*

Mini-Stories of Renewal

✨ **The Couple Who Took Seven Steps Every Year:** On each anniversary, they walked seven steps together, recalling one vow at each step. Over decades, this ritual became a sacred tradition for their children to witness.

✿ **The Annual Vow Letter:** One husband wrote to his wife every anniversary, highlighting how he saw her fulfill the vows. His wife said, *"Those letters are my treasure chest of love."*

💡 **Renewal in Tough Times:** During a health crisis, a couple renewed their vows privately in the hospital room. They realized vows matter most when life tests them.

Practical Tools

- **Vows Journal:** A shared notebook where couples jot down examples of living each vow.
- **Reminder Tokens:** Wear matching bracelets or rings that symbolize renewal.
- **Digital Vows Calendar:** Set monthly reminders to discuss one vow at a time.

Reflection Questions

1. When was the last time we spoke or reflected on our vows?
2. What ritual of renewal excites us most?
3. How do we adapt vows to our current life stage (newlyweds, parents, retirees)?
4. Which vow do we most need to strengthen this year?

Write your reflections below.

Commitment Exercise

Create your own Renewal Ritual. Example: *"Every year on our anniversary, we will light a candle, walk seven steps together, and rewrite our vows for the year ahead."*

Keep it simple but consistent—what matters is the repetition, not grandeur.

Closing Thought

Renewal is the secret to lifelong love. The vows spoken once in youth gain new meaning in middle age, and deeper resonance in old age. By revisiting them, couples remind themselves:

- Love is not a one-time promise.
- It is a living choice, renewed daily.

When couples actively renew their vows, marriage stops being routine and becomes a sacred journey—ever fresh, ever alive, ever committed.

Chapter – 13

Navigating Extended Family and Intercaste Marriages Through the Seven Vows

Marriage is not only the union of two individuals—it is often the merging of two families, two cultures, and sometimes two very different worlds. While the seven vows guide the couple's relationship, they also provide wisdom to navigate external dynamics like extended family expectations, intercaste or interfaith unions, and cultural differences.

In today's world, couples often find that honoring each other is easier than managing the opinions, traditions, and pressures of others. This chapter shows how the vows can be applied beyond the couple—to sustain harmony with families and across cultures.

Extended Family Challenges

- **Parental Expectations:** Parents may want control over finances, child-rearing, or living arrangements.
- **Generational Gaps:** Different values between elders and the couple (e.g., gender roles, career priorities).
- **Interference in Conflicts:** Family members taking sides can worsen disputes.
- **Joint vs. Nuclear Setup:** Living together can cause tension, while living apart may be seen as neglect.

❢ **Story – The Living Arrangement Conflict:** After marriage, Radhika and Kunal moved into his parents' home. His mother expected Radhika to follow traditional household roles. Kunal felt torn between loyalty to his wife and his family. Eventually, they sat with elders and explained: *"Our bond will be stronger if we also have independence."* They shifted to a nearby apartment but visited daily. This compromise honored both the marriage and family ties.

Intercaste and Interfaith Marriages

Intercaste and interfaith marriages often bring added beauty—two cultures blending—but also added strain due to societal judgments.

- **Cultural Rituals:** Deciding which traditions to follow during weddings, festivals, and child-rearing.
- **Family Resistance:** Some families may resist or disapprove.
- **Identity Confusion:** Children may feel torn between cultures.

💡 **Story – The Blended Wedding:** Priya, a Hindu, and Armaan, a Muslim, wanted to respect both traditions. Their wedding included *saat phere* around the fire and a *nikaah* under Islamic rites. Later, they raised children with exposure to both faiths. They explained: *"Our vows are not bound by one tradition—they are strengthened by two."*

Applying the Seven Vows to Extended Family and Intercaste Challenges

1. **First Vow – Nourishment & Stability**
    - Manage finances independently to reduce family conflicts.
    - Prioritize emotional stability in the couple over external approval.
2. **Second Vow – Emotional & Spiritual Support**
    - Stand united when facing criticism from family or society.
    - Support each other in balancing loyalty to families without compromising marriage.
3. **Third Vow – Discipline & Action**
    - Create clear boundaries (e.g., private couple time, decision-making authority).
    - Take proactive steps to honor both families without losing individuality.
4. **Fourth Vow – Resilience in Setbacks**
    - When family conflicts arise, avoid blame. Treat them as shared challenges.
    - Use counseling or mediation when conflicts become overwhelming.

5. **Fifth Vow – Purpose & Legacy**
    - Focus on the bigger picture—raising compassionate children and building a meaningful life—rather than winning arguments with relatives.

6. **Sixth Vow – Nurturing Family**
    - Redefine "family" as chosen bonds too—mentoring, friendships, and supportive communities.
    - For intercaste couples, teach children pride in both heritages.

7. **Seventh Vow – Companionship & Friendship**
    - Remember that the ultimate loyalty is to each other. Family systems may shift, but companionship remains constant.

Psychological Insights

- **Boundary Theory:** Healthy couples create boundaries with families—respectful yet firm.
- **Cultural Intelligence (CQ):** The ability to respect and integrate different cultural traditions strengthens intercaste marriages.
- **Family Systems Approach:** When one part of the family changes (e.g., intercaste union), others may resist. Adaptation takes time.

Reflection Questions

1. Do we stand united when family pressures challenge our bond?
2. How do we balance respect for elders with independence as a couple?
3. If from different backgrounds, how do we celebrate both cultures with pride?
4. What family traditions do we want to carry forward, and which do we want to redefine?

Write your reflections below.

Couple's Exercises

1. **Boundary Map:** Together, list areas where family can be involved (festivals, celebrations) and areas that remain couple-only (finances, parenting decisions).
2. **Culture Fusion Journal:** For intercaste couples, create a journal of blended traditions (recipes, rituals, stories). Pass it on as a legacy for children.
3. **Family Gratitude Practice:** Each week, name one thing you appreciate about your extended family—even if conflicts exist. Gratitude reduces resentment.
4. **Support Statements:** Write affirmations such as: *"We stand together when others misunderstand us."* Display them in your home.

Mini-Stories

✨ **The Sunday Lunch Rule:** One couple promised families that every Sunday was for family lunch, but weekdays were for themselves. This compromise built peace.

🏵 **The Festival Fusion:** An intercaste couple celebrated Diwali with diyas and Eid with feasts, teaching children that diversity is richness, not division.

❢ **The Supportive Parents:** An elderly father told his son: *"I may not understand your choice, but I see your happiness. That is enough for me."* Love, even when reluctant, eventually softened resistance.

Closing Thought

Extended family and intercaste challenges test the resilience of vows. Yet, when couples approach them with unity, respect, and creativity, these challenges can deepen rather than weaken love.

The seven vows remind us that loyalty begins with the couple but radiates outward with compassion. When nurtured well, a marriage becomes not only a union of two hearts but a bridge between families, cultures, and generations.

Chapter – 14

Modern Rituals and Alternative Ways to Express the Seven Vows

The seven vows of marriage are ancient in origin, but their wisdom is timeless. Today's couples, however, live in a world of fast schedules, blended cultures, and evolving expectations. While not every couple may connect to traditional rituals, every couple can reinterpret the essence of the vows through **modern, meaningful practices.**

This chapter explores alternative ways couples can **express, embody, and celebrate** their vows—making them not just memories of a wedding day but living traditions for everyday life.

Why Modern Rituals Matter

- **Accessibility:** Not all couples may marry with full rituals (civil marriages, intercaste or international unions).
- **Personalization:** Modern couples want rituals that reflect their unique love story.
- **Continuity:** Renewal rituals keep vows alive beyond anniversaries.

☞ **Insight:** Rituals are not about formality—they are about meaning. When couples design their own, the vows become deeply personal.

Modern Interpretations of Each Vow

1. **First Vow – Nourishment and Stability**
   - **Modern Ritual:** Cook a meal together once a week, symbolizing shared nourishment.

- **Alternative Symbol:** A shared piggy bank or digital savings account where both contribute equally.

2. **Second Vow – Emotional and Spiritual Support**
   - **Modern Ritual:** Begin or end the day with a 5-minute check-in.
   - **Alternative Symbol:** Lighting a candle during deep conversations as a reminder of honesty and presence.

3. **Third Vow – Self-Discipline and Action**
   - **Modern Ritual:** Set couple goals (fitness, finances, projects) and track progress together.
   - **Alternative Symbol:** A joint calendar marking shared commitments.

4. **Fourth Vow – Resilience in Setbacks**
   - **Modern Ritual:** During hard times, create a "resilience mantra" and repeat it together daily.
   - **Alternative Symbol:** A jar of notes documenting struggles overcome—reminders of shared strength.

5. **Fifth Vow – Purposeful Living and Legacy**
   - **Modern Ritual:** Volunteer together once a year or adopt a social cause as a couple.
   - **Alternative Symbol:** Planting a tree each anniversary to symbolize legacy.

6. **Sixth Vow – Nurturing Family and Children**
   - **Modern Ritual:** Create family nights with storytelling, games, or rituals of gratitude.
   - **Alternative Symbol:** A family vision board capturing shared values and dreams.
7. **Seventh Vow – Lifelong Companionship and Friendship**
   - **Modern Ritual:** Keep a "friendship journal" of inside jokes, adventures, and memories.
   - **Alternative Symbol:** A shared playlist that grows with every year, reflecting the soundtrack of their journey.

Alternative Ceremony Ideas for Diverse Couples

1. **Interfaith Marriages:** Blend traditions: take seven steps around both a sacred fire and another cultural symbol (like exchanging rings or signing a contract).
2. **Civil Marriages:** Create personal vows based on the seven principles and speak them during the ceremony.
3. **Anniversary Rituals:** Every year, revisit one vow and plan activities around it (e.g., year one: nourishment → cooking class; year two: resilience → hiking challenge).
4. **Long-Distance Marriages:** Use technology—record video vows, exchange digital "garlands" like personalized messages or e-cards.

Mini-Stories of Modern Rituals

✨ **The Dinner Table Vows:** One couple, unable to afford a traditional wedding, wrote the seven vows on slips of paper and read them aloud over dinner. Years later, they still revisit the same slips annually.

✿ **The Travel Vows:** A couple passionate about travel decided to take seven trips in their first decade of marriage, dedicating each trip to one vow. Their scrapbook became their sacred text.

💡 **The Digital Vows:** A tech-savvy pair built a shared Google Doc titled *Our Seven Vows.* They update it yearly with notes, reflections, and photos.

Psychological Insights

- **Rituals Create Anchors:** Couples who establish rituals feel more secure in times of stress.
- **Personalization Increases Commitment:** When vows are reinterpreted in unique ways, couples feel deeper ownership of them.
- **Shared Meaning (Gottman):** Strong marriages are built on rituals that express values and purpose.

Reflection Questions

1. What ritual would make the vows more alive in our daily life?
2. Which vow do we want to design a special ceremony for this year?
3. How can we blend our cultural or personal traditions into vow renewal?
4. Do our current rituals reflect who we are as a couple today?

Write your reflections below.

Couple's Exercises

1. **Create Your Own Ritual:** Choose one vow and invent a ritual around it (e.g., lighting a candle for support, planting a sapling for legacy).
2. **Seven-Year Renewal:** Every seven years, hold a private or public vow renewal. Re-speak the vows in your own words.
3. **Vow Box:** Write personal interpretations of each vow on cards and place them in a decorated box. Open it whenever you feel disconnected.
4. **Anniversary Challenge:** Dedicate each anniversary to one vow, celebrating it with an activity or reflection.

Closing Thought

The seven vows may have been spoken centuries ago, but they are not frozen in time. Their wisdom adapts to every era, every culture, and every couple willing to live them.

Modern rituals remind us that vows are not limited to a fire ceremony—they can be lived in kitchens, workplaces, gardens, or even through digital screens. When couples find creative, meaningful ways to embody them, marriage becomes not just a tradition but a living art.

Chapter – 15

Real-Life Case Studies of Couples Living (or Struggling With) the Seven Vows

The seven vows are not abstract—they come alive in the choices couples make each day. Some couples embody them beautifully, turning challenges into opportunities. Others struggle, sometimes forgetting the vows in the chaos of modern life.

This chapter shares stories—both inspiring and cautionary—that show how the vows play out in reality.

Case Study 1: The First Vow – Nourishment and Stability

✨ **A Couple That Thrived:** Rohit and Shalini both worked demanding jobs. Instead of fighting over household chores, they created a "meal-sharing system." Whoever came home earlier cooked, while the other cleaned. They also started a joint savings plan. Their sense of teamwork nourished their bond and provided emotional and financial stability.

● **A Couple That Struggled:** Ankit earned well but never discussed finances with his wife, Sneha. She felt excluded and insecure. Over time, mistrust built up. Their silence around money eroded stability, proving that provision without communication is incomplete.

Case Study 2: The Second Vow – Emotional and Spiritual Support

✨ **A Couple That Thrived:** After a miscarriage, Neel and Aarti grieved differently—he stayed quiet, she cried openly. Instead of drifting apart, they chose therapy together. Aarti later said, *"He didn't fix my pain, but he sat with me in it."* Their support deepened intimacy.

● **A Couple That Struggled:** When Simran faced postpartum depression, her husband dismissed it as "mood swings." His lack of empathy created distance. Years later, she said, *"I felt more alone in marriage than before it."*

Case Study 3: The Third Vow – Discipline and Action

✨ **A Couple That Thrived:** Pooja and Arjun created a rule: 15 minutes of couple time daily, no matter what. It seemed small, but over years it built trust and consistency. Their children later remarked, *"We always saw them prioritizing each other."*

● **A Couple That Struggled:** Vikram promised his wife weekly date nights but canceled often for work. She felt secondary to his job. His inconsistency made her stop expecting effort, weakening their bond.

Case Study 4: The Fourth Vow – Resilience in Setbacks

✨ **A Couple That Thrived:** Ramesh was diagnosed with cancer. His wife, Jyoti, became his pillar—managing treatments, encouraging positivity, and celebrating small wins. He survived, and they described the illness as *"the storm that made us unshakable."*

● **A Couple That Struggled:** When Saurabh lost his job, he withdrew emotionally. His wife, Kriti, blamed him for their financial struggles. Instead of resilience, blame took over. Within two years, they separated.

Case Study 5: The Fifth Vow – Purpose and Legacy

✨ **A Couple That Thrived:** Ravi and Lata, both teachers, mentored underprivileged children on weekends. Their purpose went beyond their careers. Their children grew up witnessing service as a way of life. Their legacy became not just biological but societal.

● **A Couple That Struggled:** A wealthy couple focused only on material success—cars, luxury, parties. Their children grew up anxious, with no sense of values. Years later, the parents admitted, *"We left them inheritance but not guidance."*

Case Study 6: The Sixth Vow – Nurturing Family and Children

✨ **A Couple That Thrived:** Deepa and Manish created a family tradition—Friday "story nights." Their children not only bonded with parents but also absorbed values through tales. Decades later, those nights remained cherished memories.

● **A Couple That Struggled:** Sunita and Raj constantly argued about parenting—she pushed for academics, he for sports. Their child grew up stressed, feeling torn between parents. Their failure to align weakened both the child's confidence and the marriage.

Case Study 7: The Seventh Vow – Lifelong Companionship

✨ **A Couple That Thrived:** An elderly couple, married 55 years, was asked their secret. The husband smiled: *"She is my best friend. We still laugh at the same silly jokes."* Friendship carried their marriage long after beauty and youth faded.

● **A Couple That Struggled:** Maya and Karan built their marriage only on attraction. Once the passion faded, they realized they had little companionship. Without shared hobbies, humor, or friendship, they drifted apart.

Lessons from Case Studies

- **Thriving couples:** Consistency, communication, empathy, and shared purpose.
- **Struggling couples:** Silence, neglect, blame, and misaligned expectations.
- **Key Insight:** The vows are not automatically kept—they require conscious renewal.

Reflection Questions

1. Which couple's story resonates most with our relationship?
2. Do we see ourselves in the thriving examples or the struggling ones?
3. Which vow do we need to re-commit to most urgently?

Write your reflections below.

Couple's Exercise – Case Study Reflection

1. Read one thriving and one struggling story together.
2. Discuss: What did the thriving couple do differently?
3. Decide: What one action can we adopt from their example?

Closing Thought

Every marriage is a case study in progress. Some couples live the vows with grace, others struggle, and most fall somewhere in between. The beauty lies not in perfection but in awareness.

By reflecting on real stories, couples see that the vows are not abstract—they are lived in choices as simple as sharing a meal, listening with empathy, or laughing together. Every day is a new chance to write your own case study of love.

Chapter – 16

A Guide for Couples to Create Their Own Personalized Vows

The seven vows are a sacred foundation, but every couple's love story is unique. Just as no two fingerprints are the same, no two marriages are identical. Creating personalized vows allows couples to honor tradition while weaving in their own promises—reflecting their personalities, struggles, and shared dreams.

This chapter is a guide to help couples **adapt the seven vows into their own language and life context.**

Why Personalize Vows?

- **Authenticity:** Words spoken from the heart feel alive.
- **Relevance:** Personalized vows reflect modern realities—dual careers, long-distance, shared parenting.
- **Connection:** Speaking vows in your own language deepens emotional intimacy.
- **Renewal:** Couples can revisit and rewrite vows as their journey evolves.

☞ **Insight:** Personalized vows don't replace the traditional ones—they *reimagine* them for today.

Steps to Crafting Personalized Vows

1. **Reflect on Your Story**
    - How did we meet?
    - What struggles have we overcome?
    - What do I admire most in my partner?
    - What do I hope we build together?

✨ **Exercise:** Journal individually, then share your reflections.

2. **Draw Inspiration from the Seven Vows**

Each traditional vow can be translated into modern terms:

- **First Vow (Nourishment):** "I promise to share responsibilities—whether cooking a meal or building our savings."
- **Second Vow (Support):** "I promise to be your safe space, especially when the world feels heavy."
- **Third Vow (Discipline):** "I promise to show up, even on days I feel tired, because you matter."
- **Fourth Vow (Resilience):** "I promise to stand with you in storms, not walk away."

- **Fifth Vow (Purpose):** “I promise to live meaningfully with you, leaving footprints of love behind.”
- **Sixth Vow (Family):** “I promise to nurture our children and honor our families with dignity.”
- **Seventh Vow (Companionship):** “I promise to remain not only your partner but also your best friend.”

3. Use Your Own Voice

- Some couples prefer poetic language.
- Others prefer simple, everyday words.
- There is no “right style”—only authentic expression.

❢ **Tip:** Write as if speaking directly to your partner, not an audience.

4. Keep It Balanced

Each partner should craft vows that reflect both giving and receiving, independence and togetherness.

5. Practice and Revise

Read them aloud privately—do they feel true, or exaggerated? Adjust until they feel natural.

Formats for Personalized Vows

1. **Traditional Adaptation:** Keep the structure of the seven vows but rewrite in modern words.

2. **Free Expression:** Write vows as love letters.

3. **Creative Symbolism:** Use metaphors: "I promise to be the lighthouse when you feel lost at sea."

4. **Shared Vows:** Write one joint vow together and speak it in unison.

Mini-Stories of Personalized Vows

✨ **The Practical Vows:** One couple wrote: *"I vow to do laundry without complaining. I vow to make you tea when you're stressed."* Their vows made guests laugh—but also captured love in daily gestures.

✿ **The Poetic Vows:** Another couple wrote in verse, describing love as seasons—*"I will be your spring of hope, your summer of joy, your autumn of wisdom, your winter of rest."*

❢ **The Blended Vows:** An intercaste couple combined traditions, adding: *"I vow to honor both our cultures and raise children proud of both heritages."*

Sample Personalized Vows

- "I promise to laugh at your silly jokes, even when I've heard them a hundred times."

- "I promise to fight fair, to listen more than I speak, and to apologize quickly."

- "I promise to choose us, again and again, even on hard days."
- "I promise to make our home not perfect, but always full of love."

Reflection Questions

1. What three qualities do I most admire in my partner?
2. What fears do I want to ease through my promises?
3. What do I want our children or future generations to know about our bond?
4. How can my vows reflect both tradition and individuality?

Write your reflections below.

Couple's Exercises

1. **Vows Worksheet:** Write one promise for each of the seven vows in your own words.

2. **Anniversary Rewrite:** Every year, rewrite your vows reflecting your growth. Keep the old ones as milestones.

3. **Vows Jar:** Write short promises on slips (e.g., "I promise to always dance with you in the kitchen"). Pull one out whenever connection feels low.

4. **Public or Private Renewal:** Decide if you want to share vows in a ceremony, or keep them intimate.

Closing Thought

Personalized vows are love spoken in your own voice. They are not only for the wedding day but for every season of life. By writing, revisiting, and renewing them, couples remind each other:

"Our love is not borrowed from tradition. It is our own story, written daily, promised freely, and lived fully."

Chapter – 17

The Role of Forgiveness and Healing in Honoring the Vows

Every couple enters marriage with love and hope, but life brings misunderstandings, disappointments, and hurt. Even the strongest bonds experience cracks. The **seven vows** are not broken by mistakes but by the refusal to forgive, heal, and move forward.

Forgiveness is not forgetting the hurt—it is choosing love over resentment. Healing is not instant—it is the slow rebuilding of trust, compassion, and connection. Together, they allow couples to honor their vows even after pain.

Why Forgiveness Matters in Marriage

- **Imperfection is Inevitable:** No partner is flawless; mistakes are part of intimacy.
- **Resentment is Poison:** Holding grudges erodes companionship faster than external challenges.
- **Forgiveness Restores Balance:** It shifts focus from "me vs. you" to "us vs. the problem."

☞ **Insight:** Forgiveness is less about the other person and more about protecting one's own heart from bitterness.

Different Kinds of Hurt in Marriage

1. **Everyday Hurts** – harsh words, neglecting small needs, forgetting special days.
2. **Betrayals of Trust** – dishonesty, financial secrecy, broken promises.

3. **Major Wounds** – infidelity, abandonment, emotional or physical abuse.

Each requires different levels of healing, but all begin with the willingness to listen, understand, and rebuild.

Real-Life Stories of Forgiveness

✨ **The Forgotten Anniversary:** Anjali was furious when her husband forgot their 10th anniversary. At first, she wanted to punish him with silence. Instead, she expressed her hurt directly. He planned a surprise dinner later that week, admitting his mistake. Over time, she chose forgiveness, realizing the relationship mattered more than one missed date.

✿ **The Business Failure:** Raj invested family savings in a failed business without consulting his wife. She felt betrayed. Through counseling, he acknowledged the breach of trust, and she gradually forgave. Later, they created a joint financial plan to ensure transparency.

❢ **The Affair:** Infidelity left Neha devastated. At first, she wanted divorce. But her husband showed genuine remorse, sought therapy, and rebuilt trust over years. She eventually forgave, not to erase the past but to free herself from bitterness. Today, they describe their bond as *"reborn, not repaired."*

The Psychology of Forgiveness

- **Empathy:** Seeing the mistake through the partner's perspective reduces anger.
- **Letting Go of Control:** Forgiveness acknowledges we cannot rewrite the past.
- **Self-Healing:** Studies show forgiving reduces stress, lowers blood pressure, and improves mental health.
- **Boundaries + Forgiveness:** True forgiveness does not mean tolerating repeated harm. Boundaries ensure safety while healing.

Practical Steps to Forgiveness

1. **Acknowledge the Hurt:** Pretending nothing happened only deepens wounds.
2. **Express Honestly:** Share your feelings without blame. Use "I feel" instead of "You always."
3. **Seek Understanding:** Ask why the mistake happened—was it ignorance, stress, or deeper conflict?
4. **Rebuild Trust Gradually:** Trust is earned through consistent actions over time.
5. **Choose Letting Go:** Forgiveness is not condoning but choosing peace over punishment.

Reflection Questions

1. What small resentments am I holding that I can release today?
2. Has my partner apologized in ways I recognize? Have I?
3. What boundaries do we need to prevent repeated hurts?
4. How does forgiveness strengthen our ability to live the vows?

Write your reflections below.

Couple's Healing Practices

1. **The Apology Ritual:** Practice sincere apologies—acknowledge, express regret, and state corrective action.
2. **Healing Letters:** Each partner writes a letter—one expressing hurt, the other expressing remorse. Exchange and discuss with compassion.
3. **Forgiveness Meditation:** Sit together, breathe deeply, and silently repeat: *"I release the past. I choose love."*
4. **Weekly Healing Talk:** Set aside time weekly to share unresolved hurts in a safe, calm setting.

Mini-Stories of Healing

✨ **The Couple Who Chose Therapy:** When constant fights drained them, a couple sought counseling. Through guided conversations, they healed years of suppressed hurt. Today, they say therapy was their "second marriage."

✿ **The Forgiveness Diary:** One wife began journaling each time she forgave her husband for small things. Later, when a bigger conflict arose, she showed him the diary. He was overwhelmed by her patience and resolved to change his habits.

💡 **The Elderly Couple's Wisdom:** When asked their secret to 50 years of marriage, they said: *"Two words—let go."*

Closing Thought

The seven vows are not promises of perfection—they are commitments to growth. Mistakes will come, but forgiveness and healing transform them into lessons rather than endings.

To forgive is to honor love over ego. To heal is to honor tomorrow over yesterday. Together, forgiveness and healing keep the vows alive—not as fragile words, but as living strength in the face of human imperfection.

Chapter - 18

Communication as the Lifeline of the Vows

Every marriage begins with promises, but those promises survive only through communication. The seven vows speak of nourishment, support, resilience, and companionship—but without words, listening, and expression, the vows fade into silence.

Communication is the oxygen of marriage. Without it, love suffocates. With it, even the most difficult seasons become bearable.

Why Communication is Central to the Vows

- **First Vow (Nourishment):** Couples must talk about financial goals and daily responsibilities.
- **Second Vow (Support):** Emotional support requires words, empathy, and active listening.
- **Third Vow (Discipline):** Discipline fails when promises are spoken but not communicated clearly.
- **Fourth Vow (Resilience):** Resilience grows when couples share fears and hopes openly.
- **Fifth Vow (Purpose):** Purpose and legacy require conversations about meaning.
- **Sixth Vow (Family):** Parenting and family care collapse without shared communication.
- **Seventh Vow (Companionship):** Friendship thrives on conversation, jokes, and shared stories.

☞ **Insight:** Every vow depends on communication to become real.

Barriers to Healthy Communication

1. **Assumptions:** Believing your partner "should just know."
2. **Defensiveness:** Responding to every concern as criticism.
3. **Interruptions:** Talking more to reply than to understand.
4. **Technology:** Scrolling while your partner is speaking.
5. **Silence in Conflict:** Withdrawing instead of resolving.

Real-Life Stories of Communication

✨ **The Tea Conversations:** Ritu and Arjun had a ritual: every evening, they drank tea together without phones. This became their space for sharing everything—work stress, children's issues, dreams. Ritu said, *"Our tea time saved our marriage."*

✿ **The Silence That Hurt:** Priya often felt her husband was distant. He insisted he loved her, but never expressed it. Over years, the silence became heavier than arguments. She later said, *"It wasn't what he did—it was what he never said."*

❢ **The Apology That Healed:** After a heated fight, a husband wrote his wife a heartfelt letter instead of waiting for the right words. That letter became their turning point, reminding them that expression matters more than pride.

The Psychology of Communication

- **Active Listening:** True listening means hearing emotions behind words.
- **Non-Verbal Communication:** Tone, touch, and eye contact often speak louder than words.
- **Love Languages (Gary Chapman):** People communicate love differently—words, acts, gifts, touch, or time.
- **Conflict Styles:** Understanding whether a partner avoids, competes, or compromises helps resolve conflicts.

Healthy Communication Practices

1. **Statements:** Replace blame ("You never listen") with responsibility ("I feel unheard when…").
2. **Mirroring:** Repeat back what your partner said to confirm understanding.
3. **Scheduled Talks:** Dedicate weekly time to discuss sensitive topics like finances or parenting.
4. **Affectionate Words:** Use daily affirmations—"thank you," "I love you," "I'm proud of you."

Reflection Questions

1. Do we truly listen, or only wait for our turn to speak?
2. What unspoken words have we avoided out of fear or pride?
3. How often do we express admiration or gratitude out loud?
4. Which of our daily rituals strengthen communication most?

Write your reflections below.

Couple's Exercises

1. **Daily Three:** Each night, share three things: one joy, one struggle, one hope.
2. **Listening Game:** One partner speaks for 2 minutes, the other only listens, then summarizes. Switch roles.
3. **Compliment Circle:** Spend 5 minutes exchanging compliments without deflection.
4. **Conflict Pause:** During arguments, agree to pause for 10 minutes, then resume calmly.

Mini-Stories of Communication

✨ **The Text Messages:** One long-distance couple sustained their bond through daily morning and night texts. Years later, they still cherish those messages as proof that words can bridge distance.

🌸 **The Storytelling Couple:** A couple began sharing one childhood story every weekend. Over time, they discovered new sides of each other—even decades into marriage.

❢ **The Whisper Ritual:** An elderly couple whispered blessings into each other's ear every night before sleep. Simple words, spoken consistently, became their sacred communication ritual.

Closing Thought

Communication is not only about talking—it is about connecting. A marriage does not collapse because of differences, but because of silence. Words spoken with love can heal wounds, resolve conflicts, and keep vows alive.

The seven vows are powerful promises, but communication is their lifeline. When couples keep talking, keep listening, and keep expressing, their vows remain more than rituals—they become living, breathing truths of their marriage.

Chapter – 19

Intimacy and Romance as Expressions of the Vows

When couples take the seven vows, they promise nourishment, support, resilience, and companionship. But these promises must also be expressed through **intimacy and romance.**

Intimacy is more than physical closeness—it is the **deep knowing, trust, and affection** between partners. Romance is not only grand gestures—it is the **daily tenderness** that keeps love alive. Together, they transform vows from spoken words into lived experiences.

The Layers of Intimacy

1. **Emotional Intimacy**
    - Sharing fears, dreams, vulnerabilities.
    - Feeling seen, heard, and accepted.
2. **Physical Intimacy**
    - Touch, affection, sexual closeness.
    - The language of the body expressing love.
3. **Intellectual Intimacy**
    - Exchanging ideas, learning together.
    - Respecting each other's thoughts.
4. **Spiritual Intimacy**
    - Praying, meditating, or reflecting together.
    - Feeling united in higher purpose.

☞ **Insight:** Couples who nurture all layers of intimacy live the vows more fully.

How Romance Keeps Vows Alive

- **First Vow (Nourishment):** Cooking together can become a romantic act.
- **Second Vow (Support):** A gentle hug after a long day can heal more than words.
- **Third Vow (Discipline):** Planning date nights shows consistent effort.
- **Fourth Vow (Resilience):** Loving gestures during tough times keep hope alive.
- **Fifth Vow (Purpose):** Romance reminds couples why they chose each other in the first place.
- **Sixth Vow (Family):** Children learn about love from watching their parents' affection.
- **Seventh Vow (Companionship):** Romance fuels friendship with playfulness.

Real-Life Stories of Intimacy and Romance

✨ **The Lunchbox Note:** Every morning, Kavita packed her husband's lunch with a small handwritten note. Sometimes funny, sometimes loving. Years later, he still saved them in a box.

✿ **The Candle Ritual:** A couple lit a candle during dinner once a week, even when exhausted. The glow reminded them of the sacredness of their bond.

❢ **The Elderly Couple's Walks:** In their seventies, one couple still held hands on evening walks. Their children said, *"Their touch speaks more than words."*

Psychology of Intimacy and Romance

- **Oxytocin Effect:** Touch releases the "bonding hormone," deepening trust.
- **Playfulness:** Shared laughter is one of the strongest predictors of long-term satisfaction.
- **Rituals of Connection (Gottman):** Daily small gestures matter more than rare grand ones.
- **Attachment Theory:** Secure attachment grows when couples consistently meet emotional and physical needs.

Common Barriers to Intimacy

- Stress and busy schedules.
- Unresolved conflicts.
- Misaligned sexual needs.
- Believing romance should fade with time.

☞ **Truth:** Intimacy and romance do not fade naturally—they fade when neglected.

Practical Ways to Keep Intimacy Alive

1. **Daily Affection** – Small touches, hugs, kisses.
2. **Micro-Moments of Romance** – Sending a sweet text, leaving a voice note.

3. **Date Nights** – Even at home, with simple effort.
4. **Shared Adventures** – Travel, hobbies, or new activities together.
5. **Bedroom Communication** – Honest conversations about desires and comfort.

Reflection Questions

1. Do we prioritize intimacy as much as work and chores?
2. How do we express romance in daily life?
3. Which type of intimacy (emotional, physical, spiritual, intellectual) do we need to nurture more?
4. What rituals of connection can we create to strengthen romance?

Write your reflections below.

Couple's Exercises

1. **Five-Minute Hug:** Every morning or evening, hold each other for five minutes in silence.
2. **Romance Jar:** Write small romantic ideas on slips (walk, surprise coffee, love note). Pick one weekly.
3. **Gratitude Intimacy:** Share one thing you appreciate about your partner before sleeping.
4. **Sensory Connection:** Explore non-sexual touch (holding hands, massage, forehead kisses) to build closeness.

Mini-Stories

✨ **The Surprise Playlist:** One husband created a playlist of songs from different stages of their relationship and gifted it on their anniversary. His wife said, *"It was like reliving our love story in music."*

🌸 **The Coffee Ritual:** Every Sunday morning, a couple drank coffee together before the children woke up. This sacred hour became their weekly romance.

💡 **The Long-Distance Letters:** A couple living in different cities wrote letters by hand, despite video calls. Those letters became treasures—physical symbols of love.

Closing Thought

Intimacy and romance are not luxuries in marriage—they are necessities. They turn the vows into lived experiences of love, laughter, and closeness.

When partners hold hands, whisper affection, or share quiet moments, they are not just being romantic—they are silently renewing their vows.

Chapter – 20

Conflict as a Pathway to Deeper Understanding

Many couples believe that conflict signals weakness in marriage. But the truth is, every long-term relationship faces disagreements—about money, parenting, intimacy, or family. The difference between couples who thrive and those who break is not the **presence of conflict**, but the **way conflict is handled.**

Conflict, when approached with maturity and compassion, becomes a bridge to deeper understanding. It helps couples honor the vows by revealing hidden needs, vulnerabilities, and growth opportunities.

Why Conflict Happens

1. **Different Backgrounds:** Each partner brings unique values, traditions, and habits.
2. **Unmet Needs:** Arguments often mask deeper emotional needs like respect or security.
3. **Stress and Fatigue:** External pressures spill into the relationship.
4. **Communication Gaps:** Misunderstandings escalate when partners don't feel heard.
5. **Control vs. Freedom:** Couples struggle to balance independence and togetherness.

☞ **Insight:** Beneath every conflict is a longing to feel loved, valued, and safe.

The Link Between Conflict and the Seven Vows

- **First Vow (Nourishment):** Disputes over money or chores.
- **Second Vow (Support):** Conflicts when one feels emotionally neglected.
- **Third Vow (Discipline):** Broken commitments lead to mistrust.
- **Fourth Vow (Resilience):** How couples fight during setbacks shows their true strength.
- **Fifth Vow (Purpose):** Misaligned life goals (career, children, legacy).
- **Sixth Vow (Family):** Parenting disagreements or in-law interference.
- **Seventh Vow (Companionship):** Feeling more like roommates than friends.

Conflict exposes where vows are strained—and offers a chance to renew them.

Real-Life Stories of Conflict and Growth

✨ **The Financial Argument:** Ravi wanted to save aggressively; his wife, Meera, valued experiences like travel. Their fights were endless. Finally, they created a 70-30 plan—70% for savings, 30% for enjoyment. This compromise turned tension into teamwork.

✿ **The Parenting Disagreement:** Anita believed in strict discipline; her husband, Sameer, wanted gentle parenting. After many heated arguments, they attended a parenting workshop together. Learning together not only improved parenting but also deepened respect for each other's perspectives.

❢ **The Silent Treatment:** A couple avoided conflicts by staying silent. Over years, resentment piled up until small triggers caused explosions. Through therapy, they learned that healthy conflict was safer than suppressed silence.

Healthy vs. Unhealthy Conflict

Healthy Conflict:

- Focuses on the issue, not character attacks.
- Involves listening as much as speaking.
- Ends with compromise or mutual respect.

Unhealthy Conflict:

- Includes insults, blame, or withdrawal.
- Focuses on "winning" instead of resolving.
- Leaves wounds unhealed, piling up bitterness.

Psychological Insights

- **Gottman's Research:** The "Four Horsemen" of marital breakdown—criticism, contempt, defensiveness, and stonewalling. Couples must replace these with gentle start-ups, appreciation, responsibility, and self-soothing.

- **Conflict Styles:** Competing, avoiding, accommodating, compromising, collaborating. The healthiest long-term style is *collaboration.*
- **Attachment Theory:** Insecure attachment can make partners either overly defensive or avoidant during conflict. Secure couples fight, but without fearing abandonment.

Strategies for Healthy Conflict

1. **Pause Before Reacting:** Take a breath, walk away briefly if needed.
2. **Use Gentle Start-Ups:** Begin with calm words: *"I feel worried when bills pile up"* instead of *"You're irresponsible!"*
3. **Seek Common Ground:** Focus on solutions, not who is right.
4. **Agree to Disagree:** Some differences (political views, habits) may never align. Respect matters more than agreement.
5. **Repair Quickly:** A simple apology or hug after a fight can prevent long-term damage.

Reflection Questions

1. Do we fight to win, or to understand?
2. Which recurring conflict teaches us about deeper needs?
3. How can we transform our disagreements into growth?
4. Do we resolve fights, or bury them under silence?

Write your reflections below.

Couple's Exercises

1. **Conflict Replay:** Recall your last fight. Write down what you both could have done differently.
2. **Trigger Mapping:** List common triggers (money, parenting, in-laws). Create agreed strategies for each.
3. **Safe Word Practice:** Choose a word to pause heated arguments. Example: "Lotus." Whoever says it signals time to cool down.
4. **Resolution Ritual:** After every fight, end with an act of connection—a hug, prayer, or affirmation.

Mini-Stories

✨ **The Hug Rule:** A couple promised never to sleep without hugging, no matter how angry. This ritual softened many fights.

✿ **The Whiteboard Method:** One pair wrote conflicts on a whiteboard. They erased resolved issues together, symbolizing release.

💡 **The Laughter Break:** During fights, one husband cracked silly jokes. His wife tried to stay angry but ended up laughing. They learned that humor could be a bridge.

Closing Thought

Conflict is not the opposite of love—it is an invitation to understand love more deeply. Each disagreement offers couples a chance to recommit to the vows, to learn each other's hidden needs, and to grow stronger together.

Handled with patience and respect, conflict becomes not a storm that destroys, but rain that nourishes the roots of marriage.

Chapter – 21

Parenting, Partnership, and the Seven Vows

Parenting is one of the most joyful yet challenging journeys a couple can undertake. Children bring laughter, purpose, and growth—but they also bring sleepless nights, financial strain, and endless responsibilities.

The seven vows are not just about sustaining the couple—they provide a compass for raising children with love and unity. When partners parent as a team, they not only nurture their children but also honor their vows in action.

Parenting Through the Lens of the Seven Vows

1. **First Vow – Nourishment and Stability**
   - Ensuring children have food, shelter, and safety.
   - Financial planning for education and future needs.
   - Teaching children the value of balance between needs and wants.

2. **Second Vow – Emotional and Spiritual Support**
   - Being present for a child's fears, joys, and questions.
   - Guiding them in faith, ethics, or values.
   - Standing united as parents when children face challenges.

3. **Third Vow – Discipline and Action**
   - Teaching discipline by example, not only rules.
   - Consistency in routines—bedtime, study, play.
   - Showing children that love and structure can coexist.

4. **Fourth Vow – Resilience in Setbacks**
   - Supporting children through failures and struggles.
   - Modeling perseverance during crises.
   - Teaching them to bounce back, not fear mistakes.

5. **Fifth Vow – Purpose and Legacy**
   - Instilling purpose, service, and vision in children.
   - Passing on cultural, moral, or spiritual heritage.
   - Building not only careers for them but character within them.

6. **Sixth Vow – Nurturing Family and Community**
   - Creating a home where children feel safe and loved.
   - Teaching respect for grandparents, relatives, and community.
   - Encouraging empathy and kindness in daily life.

7. **Seventh Vow – Lifelong Companionship**
    - Showing children what love looks like by modeling companionship.
    - Reminding them that a strong partnership is the foundation of family stability.
    - Creating family traditions that bind generations.

Real-Life Parenting Stories

✨ **The Bedtime Readers:** One couple read stories to their children every night. Years later, the children credited this ritual for their love of learning and closeness with parents.

✿ **The United Front:** When their teenage son rebelled, parents Ankit and Reema initially disagreed—one wanted strictness, the other leniency. After many fights, they decided to discuss privately first and present a united stance. Their son eventually respected their consistency.

❢ **The Strained Marriage:** A couple poured all energy into children but neglected their relationship. After years, they realized they had grown apart. Therapy reminded them that parenting works best when partnership thrives.

Parenting Challenges and the Vows

1. **Sleep Deprivation and Stress:** Couples must support each other instead of blaming.
2. **Different Parenting Styles:** Balance discipline with nurturing through dialogue.
3. **Work-Life Balance:** Protect family time from being consumed by careers.
4. **Teenage Years:** Remember resilience and patience when children test limits.
5. **Empty Nest:** When children grow up, companionship remains the anchor.

Psychological Insights

- **Attachment Theory:** Securely attached children are raised by parents who are emotionally available.
- **Parenting Styles:** Authoritative parenting (firm yet loving) produces the healthiest outcomes.
- **Modeling:** Children learn more from observing their parents' relationship than from lectures.

Reflection Questions

1. Do we model the values we want our children to adopt?
2. How can we divide parenting tasks to avoid imbalance?
3. Are we prioritizing our partnership as much as parenting?
4. What traditions will our children remember 20 years from now?

Write your reflections below.

Couple's Practices for Parenting

1. **Parenting Meetings:** Schedule weekly check-ins to discuss children's needs, keeping disagreements out of earshot.
2. **Divide and Rotate:** Share tasks (school runs, bedtime) fairly. Rotate to avoid burnout.
3. **Date Nights Without Guilt:** Show children that parental love is as important as parental care.
4. **Family Rituals:** Weekly traditions (meals, games, gratitude circles) create stability.

Mini-Stories

✨ **The Gratitude Jar:** One family placed a jar in the living room where everyone added a note of gratitude daily. On New Year's Eve, they read them aloud together.

✿ **The Kitchen Conversations:** A mother and father cooked dinner with their children every Sunday. Those evenings became the family's sacred bonding time.

❗ **The Empty Nest Realization:** When their children moved abroad, a couple realized their marriage had been child-centered. They began to date again, rediscovering companionship.

Closing Thought

Parenting is not separate from the seven vows—it is their living expression. Children do not only inherit wealth or education; they inherit the values, traditions, and love patterns they observe.

When couples parent as partners, they create not only strong families but also future generations who understand the true meaning of the vows.

Chapter – 22

Balancing Individuality and Togetherness in Marriage

Marriage is a dance of two souls—sometimes in perfect rhythm, sometimes stepping on each other's toes. The beauty of this dance lies in learning how to stay connected without losing yourself.

Every person in marriage carries unique dreams, talents, and purposes. At the same time, marriage asks for unity, compromise, and shared goals. Balancing these two truths—*"I am me"* and *"We are us"*—is one of the deepest challenges and gifts of love.

Why Balance Matters

- **Too much individuality:** Partners may feel like roommates, drifting apart.
- **Too much togetherness:** Partners may feel suffocated, losing personal growth.
- **Healthy balance:** Partners remain connected yet free, bonded yet independent.

☞ **Insight:** A strong marriage is not about two halves becoming one, but two wholes walking together.

The Seven Vows and Balance

1. **First Vow – Nourishment**
    - Share responsibilities but allow personal ways of contributing (e.g., one cooks, one manages finances).

2. **Second Vow – Support**
   - Support each other's passions even when they differ (e.g., one loves art, the other sports).

3. **Third Vow – Discipline**
   - Maintain personal discipline (fitness, study, prayer) while respecting shared routines.

4. **Fourth Vow – Resilience**
   - In crises, stand united, but also allow space for individual coping mechanisms.

5. **Fifth Vow – Purpose**
   - Create shared goals while encouraging each partner's personal dreams.

6. **Sixth Vow – Family**
   - Parent as a team, but also keep individual bonds with children.

7. **Seventh Vow – Companionship**
   - Enjoy shared hobbies but also pursue personal interests.

Real-Life Stories of Balance

✨ **The Artist and the Banker:** Anaya, a painter, needed creative freedom; her husband, Sameer, loved structured routines. Initially, they clashed. Later, they created a rhythm—he supported her exhibitions, she respected his schedules. Their differences became complementary.

✿ **The Over-Fused Couple:** Rohit and Shreya did everything together—same hobbies, same social circle. Over time, Shreya felt she had "lost herself." Only when she restarted dance classes did she regain confidence, making the marriage healthier.

❢ **The Distant Partners:** A couple focused only on careers and individual goals. They realized they had no shared rituals or hobbies. They began weekend hikes, which restored intimacy.

Psychological Insights

- **Interdependence Theory:** Healthy couples are neither dependent nor independent but interdependent—able to rely on each other while remaining whole.
- **Self-Expansion Theory:** Relationships thrive when each partner's individuality expands the other's world.
- **Boundaries in Marriage:** Respecting each other's personal space prevents resentment.

Practices for Balancing Individuality and Togetherness

1. **Personal Time, Couple Time:** Schedule both—e.g., one evening a week for individual hobbies, one for date night.
2. **Shared Growth Projects:** Learn something together (cooking, language, fitness) while also supporting solo pursuits.

3. **Respecting Differences:** Celebrate your partner's unique strengths instead of trying to mold them into yourself.

4. **Check-In Rituals:** Weekly conversations: *"How are we doing as a couple? How are you doing as an individual?"*

Reflection Questions

1. Do I encourage my partner's individuality, or do I see it as competition?

2. Are we spending enough intentional time together beyond responsibilities?

3. What shared rituals anchor us as a couple?

4. What personal passions keep me feeling whole in this marriage?

Write your reflections below.

Couple's Exercises

1. **Independence List:** Each partner writes what they need for personal growth (hobbies, friendships). Share and respect them.
2. **Togetherness Map:** Create a list of activities you love doing together. Commit to practicing them regularly.
3. **Support Statements:** Write affirmations like, *"I support your individuality because it enriches our togetherness."*
4. **Calendar Balance:** Plan a month with both solo and couple activities.

Mini-Stories

✨ **The Solo Traveler:** A wife loved solo travel once a year. Her husband initially resisted but later realized it made her return refreshed and more loving.

🌸 **The Shared Garden:** A couple with different careers found unity in gardening together every weekend. Their individuality flourished during the week, their togetherness bloomed in the garden.

💡 **The Independent Friends:** Each partner maintained separate friend circles but also nurtured a joint one. This kept social life rich and balanced.

Closing Thought

Marriage is not about losing yourself but about finding a rhythm where individuality and togetherness dance in harmony. The vows remind us that love grows best when both partners flourish—not as shadows of each other, but as shining lights walking side by side.

Conclusion Living the Seven Vows Every Day

Marriage is often celebrated on the wedding day with rituals, music, and blessings. Yet, its true beauty is revealed not in a single ceremony but in the countless ordinary days that follow—the shared meals, the small arguments, the whispered prayers, the laughter of children, the moments of silence, and the choices made together in both joy and pain.

The **seven vows** are not ancient words bound to tradition. They are timeless principles that speak to the deepest needs of every human heart: stability, support, discipline, resilience, purpose, family, and companionship.

- The **First Vow** reminds us that love begins with care—providing for one another, building stability.
- The **Second Vow** teaches us to be each other's safe space, emotionally and spiritually.
- The **Third Vow** shows that consistency and discipline protect the bond.
- The **Fourth Vow** gives us courage to face storms, knowing we are never alone.

- The **Fifth Vow** invites us to live with meaning, to create a legacy beyond ourselves.
- The **Sixth Vow** calls us to nurture family and community, weaving love into the next generation.
- The **Seventh Vow** crowns all the others—reminding us that at the heart of marriage is friendship, companionship, and lifelong partnership.

Marriage as a Journey, Not a Destination

Every couple will face moments of conflict, forgiveness, change, and renewal. At times, they may feel they are drifting apart; at others, they may feel more deeply united than ever before. What matters is the choice to **keep walking together**, honoring the vows not just once at the sacred fire, but daily—through words, actions, and intentions.

The Modern Meaning of Ancient Wisdom

This book has shown that the vows are not relics of the past. They live on when:

- Couples communicate with honesty.
- Families embrace diversity and intercaste unions with compassion.
- Individuals balance individuality and togetherness.
- Intimacy, forgiveness, and resilience transform challenges into growth.

When reinterpreted with creativity and love, the vows continue to guide not only traditional weddings but also modern partnerships, intercultural unions, and even vow renewals.

A Call to Couples

As you close this book, remember:

- Your marriage is your sacred story.
- The seven vows are your compass, not a cage.
- Love is not about perfection but about showing up, again and again, with openness and kindness.

Every day offers a new chance to nourish, support, heal, laugh, dream, and walk hand in hand.

Final Thought

The seven vows are not just promises spoken—they are choices lived. They are not only about two people—they ripple outward into families, communities, and generations.

When honored with awareness and love, these vows transform marriage into what it was always meant to be: not just a bond of duty, but a sacred partnership of hearts, souls, and lives—woven together in friendship, faith, and forever companionship.

Compatibility and Understanding Partner's Mind (Multiple Choice)

1. **Core Values and Beliefs:**

   1. **What are the most important values in your life?**
      - A) Family
      - B) Success
      - C) Freedom
      - D) Spirituality
      - E) Personal growth

   2. **How do you feel about spirituality or religion?**
      - A) It's very important to me.
      - B) It's somewhat important.
      - C) I'm open to different beliefs.
      - D) I'm not spiritual or religious.
      - E) I'm undecided about spirituality.

3. **What does success mean to you?**
   - A) Achieving financial stability
   - B) Finding happiness and balance
   - C) Building strong relationships
   - D) Gaining personal recognition
   - E) Making a difference in the world
4. **What kind of impact do you want to leave on the world?**
   - A) Help others and improve lives
   - B) Achieve professional excellence
   - C) Create something meaningful
   - D) Build a loving family
   - E) I'm not sure yet

2. **Lifestyle and Habits:**

5. **How do you like to spend your weekends?**
   - A) Relaxing at home
   - B) Being outdoors or exercising
   - C) Socializing with friends
   - D) Traveling or exploring
   - E) Working on personal projects

6. **How do you usually cope with stress?**
   - A) Talking to someone I trust
   - B) Taking time to relax
   - C) Exercising or meditating
   - D) Distracting myself with hobbies
   - E) I keep my stress to myself
7. **How would you describe your perfect day?**
   - A) Being productive and getting things done
   - B) Spending time with loved ones
   - C) Relaxing and enjoying a quiet day
   - D) Going on an adventure
   - E) Focusing on personal growth or hobbies
8. **What's your view on health and fitness?**
   - A) It's essential and part of my daily routine
   - B) I try to stay active when possible
   - C) I'm interested but not very consistent
   - D) I focus more on mental wellness than physical fitness
   - E) It's not a priority for me

3. **Financial Compatibility:**

9. **How do you manage your money?**
    - A) I like to save and invest
    - B) I spend but keep a budget
    - C) I prioritize enjoying life over saving
    - D) I'm more spontaneous with money
    - E) I leave finances to my partner
10. **What's your financial goal for the next 5 years?**
    - A) Save for a house or big purchase
    - B) Build an emergency fund
    - C) Travel or enjoy life experiences
    - D) Become debt-free
    - E) I'm still figuring out my goals
11. **How do you feel about sharing finances in a relationship?**
    - A) I'm comfortable sharing everything
    - B) I prefer to keep some independence
    - C) I'd like to combine finances partially
    - D) I'd rather keep finances separate
    - E) I haven't thought about it much

12. **What's your attitude towards debt?**
    - A) Avoid it at all costs
    - B) It's manageable if planned well
    - C) I'm okay with some debt for big goals
    - D) I don't mind taking financial risks
    - E) I'm unsure about how to handle debt

4. **Family and Relationships:**

13. **What's your vision for marriage or long-term commitment?**
    - A) It's a top priority for me
    - B) I'm open to it in the future
    - C) It's not a priority right now
    - D) I don't believe in marriage
    - E) I haven't decided yet

14. **How do you feel about having children?**
    - A) I definitely want kids
    - B) I'm open to having kids
    - C) I don't want children
    - D) I'm undecided on the topic
    - E) I'd prefer focusing on other goals

15. How involved should family be in our relationship?

- A) Very involved, family comes first
- B) Involved, but with some boundaries
- C) Limited involvement
- D) I'd prefer we focus on ourselves
- E) I'm open to compromise

16. How should we resolve conflicts?

- A) Discuss calmly and work towards a solution
- B) Take time to cool off and then talk
- C) I prefer to avoid conflict
- D) I need space before I can address issues
- E) It depends on the situation

5. Communication Style:

17. How do you prefer to communicate when something is bothering you?

- A) Talk openly and directly
- B) Take time to think before speaking
- C) I struggle with expressing myself
- D) I usually avoid confrontation
- E) I prefer to write down my thoughts

18. When you feel hurt, what do you need from me?

- A) Reassurance and comfort
- B) Space to process my feelings
- C) A calm discussion about what happened
- D) A simple apology
- E) I'm not sure yet

19. What's your love language?

- A) Words of affirmation
- B) Quality time
- C) Physical touch
- D) Acts of service
- E) Gift giving

20. What makes you feel loved and appreciated?

- A) Small acts of kindness
- B) Verbal affirmations and compliments
- C) Spending quality time together
- D) Physical affection
- E) Personal space and understanding

6. **Long-Term Vision:**

21. **Where do you see yourself in the next 5 years?**
    - A) Focused on career success
    - B) Settling down with family
    - C) Exploring new personal goals
    - D) Traveling and experiencing new things
    - E) I'm not sure yet

22. **What kind of life do you want us to build together?**
    - A) A stable, family-centered life
    - B) A balanced life with room for growth
    - C) A life full of adventure and exploration
    - D) A simple, peaceful life
    - E) I'm still figuring it out

23. **How do you balance work and life?**
    - A) I prioritize work but make time for family
    - B) I try to keep work and personal life separate
    - C) I struggle to balance the two
    - D) I prioritize personal life over work
    - E) I'm not sure what balance looks like

24. What are your non-negotiables for long-term happiness?

- A) Financial security
- B) Strong family ties
- C) Personal independence
- D) Adventure and travel
- E) Emotional support and understanding

7. Personal Growth and Development:

25. What are you currently working on improving about yourself?

- A) Building self-confidence
- B) Balancing work and life
- C) Improving communication skills
- D) Becoming healthier
- E) Finding inner peace

26. How do you feel about seeking outside help (e.g., therapy)?

- A) I’m open to it when needed
- B) I’m hesitant but would consider it
- C) I’m not comfortable with the idea
- D) I believe in solving issues independently
- E) I haven’t thought much about it

8. Social Life and Friendships:

27. How important is time with friends to you?

- A) It's very important to me
- B) I enjoy it, but balance it with other things
- C) I prefer more alone time
- D) It's not a priority for me
- E) I haven't thought much about it

28. How do you feel about personal space in a relationship?

- A) I need a lot of personal space
- B) I like a balance of togetherness and space
- C) I prefer being close most of the time
- D) I don't need much personal space
- E) I'm not sure what I need yet

9. Parental Involvement in Family Care:

29. How do you see the involvement of your parents in our family decisions?

- A) Very involved, I value their input on most matters.
- B) Involved, but with clear boundaries on important decisions.
- C) Limited involvement, I prefer to make decisions independently.
- D) They should not be involved in our family decisions.
- E) I'm open to their occasional advice.

30. How often do you expect to spend time with your parents or extended family?

- A) Frequently, as family is very important to me.
- B) Occasionally, during holidays or special events.
- C) Rarely, I prefer more time with just our immediate family.
- D) Only when absolutely necessary.
- E) I'm not sure yet.

31. How should we handle care for aging parents?

- A) We should take full responsibility for their care.
- B) We should share the responsibility with siblings and family.
- C) I prefer to seek professional care services.
- D) I believe in offering emotional support, but not direct care.
- E) We should decide based on the situation when the time comes.

32. How important is it to you that we spend time with both sides of our families equally?

- A) It's very important to me.
- B) It's somewhat important but not always necessary.
- C) I'm flexible as long as we're spending time with family.
- D) I'm okay with focusing more on one side of the family.
- E) I prefer minimal involvement with extended family.

10. Children and Parenting:

33. How do you envision raising children together?

- A) With shared responsibilities, making joint decisions.
- B) I prefer traditional roles, with one person focusing on work and the other on parenting.
- C) I see us being flexible depending on circumstances.
- D) I expect one of us to take more responsibility for raising the kids.
- E) I'm undecided about parenting roles.

34. What's your preferred approach to discipline?

- A) Structured and firm, with clear rules and consequences.
- B) Balanced, combining discipline with understanding.
- C) Gentle and flexible, letting children explore their own boundaries.
- D) I'm unsure, we can figure it out together.
- E) I'm not a strong believer in discipline.

35. How many children would you ideally like to have?

- A) None
- B) One
- C) Two
- D) Three or more
- E) I'm undecided.

36. What role do you think extended family (e.g., grandparents, aunts, uncles) should play in our children's lives?

- A) A very active role, I want them to be heavily involved.
- B) An involved role, but with clear boundaries.
- C) They should be involved only occasionally.
- D) They should have little to no involvement.
- E) I'm flexible and open to what works best.

37. What are your thoughts on education and schooling for our children?

- A) Education is the top priority, and I want them to attend the best schools.
- B) A balanced education is important, but I also value extracurricular activities.
- C) I believe in non-traditional or homeschooling approaches.
- D) I'm open to whatever suits our children best.
- E) I haven't thought about it much yet.

38. How should we divide parenting duties (e.g., feeding, bedtime, schoolwork)?

- A) We should split everything 50/50.
- B) We should alternate responsibilities based on our schedules.
- C) One of us should take the lead, with the other helping when possible.
- D) I expect to take more responsibility in certain areas.
- E) We'll figure it out as we go.

39. How do you feel about hiring help (e.g., nannies, babysitters) for childcare?

- A) I'm fully open to hiring help for our convenience.
- B) I'm comfortable with occasional help for emergencies or specific needs.
- C) I'd prefer to minimize outside help unless absolutely necessary.
- D) I don't want to involve outside help at all.
- E) I'm undecided on this matter.

40. What are your thoughts on how we should balance work and childcare?

- A) We should share the balance equally.
- B) One person should focus more on childcare, while the other works.
- C) We should adjust based on our careers and needs.
- D) I believe in outsourcing some childcare while we both focus on our work.
- E) We'll see how it works out over time.

Structure

Each section (like Core Values, Lifestyle, Finances, Family, Communication, etc.) will:

1. Each answer (A–E) will carry a **score** (e.g., 5 → very compatible, 1 → low compatibility).
2. At the end of each section, both partners will:
   - Compare answers.
   - Calculate the **compatibility percentage**.
   - Reflect on areas of agreement or potential discussion.

Scoring System Example:

Compatibility Level	Score Range	Meaning
81–100%	🌟 Excellent Compatibility	Deep understanding and shared values.
61–80%	💖 Moderate Compatibility	Minor differences, easily managed with communication.
41–60%	💬 Needs Work	Differences exist—requires honest dialogue and flexibility.
0–40%	⚠️ Low Compatibility	Major value or lifestyle gaps—seek clarity and open conversation.

Example of Interactive Use

Step 1: Both partners answer each question separately.

Step 2: Compare your responses for each item:

- If both chose the same option → 5 points
- If adjacent options → 3 points
- If opposite ends (e.g., A vs. E) → 1 point

Step 3: Add total points and divide by total possible points × 100 = **compatibility percentage**.

Notes